The New DAIRY COOKBOOK

CAXTON EDITIONS

ACKNOWLEDGMENTS

Executive Editor	Nick Rowe
Author and Food Stylist	Sue Ashworth
Managing Editor	Emily Davenport
Planning & Research	Sara-Jane Berry
Designer	Janet James
Cover Design	Open Door Limited
Photography	Steve Lee
Photographic Assistant	Tony Briscoe
Props Stylist	Helen Payne
Recipe Testing	Wendy Smith
	Serena Stubbs
	Jenny Grocott
Colour Separation	Radstock Reproductions Ltd
Print and Binding	Sunfung
	Printed in China

This edition published in 2003 by Caxton Editions
20 Bloomsbury Street
London WC1B 3JH
a member of the Caxton Publishing Group

© Eaglemoss Consumer Publications Ltd 2001

Photography © Steve Lee

Text and recipes © Sue Ashworth
Sue Ashworth has asserted her right under the
Copyright, Designs and Patents Act 1988 to be identified
as the author of this work.

Title: The New Dairy Cookbook
ISBN: 1 84067 500 4

Whilst every care has been taken in compiling the
information in this book, the publishers cannot accept
any responsibility for any errors, inadvertent or not, that
may be found or may occur at some time in the future
owing to changes in legislation or for any other reason.

CONTENTS

The New Dairy Cookbook

Writing this cook book has been a pleasure and a privilege. A pleasure, because I have always enjoyed eating dairy foods and using them to create delicious recipes. A privilege, because it really is an honour to represent the dairy industry by contributing to this beautiful book and sharing some of my favourite recipes with you. I hope that *The New Dairy Cookbook* will become a familiar and reliable friend in your kitchen, and be a source of inspiration for many memorable meals cooked in your home.

The dairy industry has a highly regarded reputation for producing some of our most attractive, best-loved and well-used cook books. *The Dairy Book of Home Cookery* – originally printed in 1968, with two subsequent editions – became a trustworthy source for reliable recipes in more than two million homes and schools throughout the country. *The Dairy Book of Family Cookery* followed, celebrating fifty years of the Milk Marketing Board in 1983, and in 1988 *The Dairy Book of British Food* commemorated British Food and Farming Year. I know that so many of these books have earned their living in your kitchens – referred to time and again for their wonderful recipes, and I hope that you agree that this book follows in their footsteps.

Quality dairy foods are part of our national heritage and they are something that we should all appreciate, for many hours of hard work are devoted to the nature and nurture of these premium foods. From fresh milk, cream, butter and yogurt to mild and mature cheeses, there is a wealth of delicious British dairy produce for you to enjoy, brought to our homes by another British institution – the milkmen and women who brave all types of weather to deliver to our doorstep. It's another

valuable part of our heritage that we should aim to hold on to.

Most of us seem to lead such busy lives these days, so much so that sometimes we hardly have time to eat, let alone cook. I think it makes it even more important to take a step back every now and then to appreciate the important things in life. Personally, I can hardly imagine anything more pleasurable than good food enjoyed in the company of good friends – closely followed by tucking into some tasty food all by myself! The essence of these recipes is that they rely on good, fresh ingredients, quite simply prepared to give really delicious results. For novice cooks – or those of you that haven't tried a particular recipe – each chapter begins with a classic dish for you to get the hang of. So if your scones leave something to be desired, or if you want to try your hand at mastering profiteroles – these recipes are for you. The remaining recipes in each chapter are clearly explained and straightforward to follow. Every recipe has been beautifully photographed to tempt you into trying it – and show you what to expect when you've finished preparing it.

Every single recipe in this book has been treble tested – firstly in its creation, secondly by the happy band of recipe testers at Milk Marque Product Development Centre in Nantwich, and thirdly in its preparation for photography – and yes, we do cook the real thing, and eat it afterwards!

So welcome to *The New Dairy Cookbook*. I trust that you, your family and your friends will enjoy this collection of wonderful dairy recipes, and I hope you are as pleased with the book as I am. Working on it has been a labour of love.

SUE ASHWORTH

Cook's Information

Metric and imperial measurements are given in all the recipes. Follow one or the other set and do not mix the two, as they are not interchangeable.

METRIC AND IMPERIAL EQUIVALENTS

Dry weight conversions

Metric	Imperial
15g	½oz
25g	1oz
40g	1½oz
50g	2oz
75g	3oz
110g	4oz (¼lb)
150g	5oz
175g	6oz
200g	7oz
225g	8oz (½lb)
250g	9oz
275g	10oz
300g	11oz
350g	12oz (¾lb)
375g	13oz
400g	14oz
425g	15oz
450g	16oz (1lb)
500g	1lb 2oz
680g	1lb 8oz
900g	2lb
1kg	2lb 4oz
1.125kg	2lb 8oz
1.25kg	2lb 12oz
1.5kg	3lb 5oz
2kg	4lb 8oz
2.25kg	5lb
2.5kg	5lb 8oz
3kg	6lb 8oz

Liquid conversions

Metric	Imperial	U.S. cups
15ml	½ floz	1 tablespoon
30ml	1 floz	⅛ cup
60ml	2 floz	¼ cup
90ml	3 floz	⅜ cup
125ml	4 floz	½ cup
150ml	5 floz (¼pt)	⅔ cup
175ml	6 floz	¾ cup
250ml	8 floz	1 cup
300ml	10 floz (½pt)	1¼ cups
375ml	12 floz	1½ cups
450ml	15 floz	1¾ cups
500ml (½ litre)	16 floz	2 cups
600ml	20 floz (1pt)	2½ cups
750ml	1¼ pints	3⅓ cups
900ml	1½ pints	3¾ cups
1 litre	1¾ pints	4 cups (1qt)
1.25 litres	2 pints	5 cups
1.5 litres	2½ pints	3 U.S. pints
2 litres	3½ pints	2 quarts

Oven temperatures

°C	°F	Gas Mark
110	225	¼
120/130	250	½
140	275	1
150	300	2
160/170	325	3
180	350	4
190	375	5
200	400	6
220	425	7
230	450	8
240	475	9

Please note that all oven temperatures vary.
Do check your manufacturer's handbook, especially if you have a fan-assisted oven.

Use a set of measuring spoons for teaspoons and tablespoons, and make sure that they are levelled off, unless otherwise stated.

1 teaspoon = 5ml
2 teaspoons = 10ml
3 teaspoons = 1 tablespoon = 15ml

All egg sizes are medium, unless otherwise stated.

soups, starters, snacks and light meals

When you want a dish that's quick and tasty, this is the chapter you'll be dipping into for inspiration. You'll find wonderful soups which burst with the flavours of fresh vegetables, delicious dairy products, herbs and seafood – there's even a fabulous chilled soup for the summer months. All the soups make perfect starters, or serve them as a light meal in their own right with fresh crusty bread and real butter.

If you fancy something a little different, there are a couple of very tasty pâtés to tempt you – so adaptable that they become dips or sandwich fillers at the stir of a spoon. Then there are some superb ways with potatoes and the most wonderful recipes using cheese. So don't just let the photographs make your mouth water – sample the real thing.

Getting the hang of...

CHEDDAR GORGEOUS SOUP

A wonderful soup with a lovely, creamy flavour. It's easy to make and uses simple, straightforward ingredients – butter, onions, stock and fresh milk, blended with soft cheese, herbs and mature Cheddar. Serve it topped with scrumptious garlic and melting Cheddar toasts.

SERVES 4

Suitable for vegetarians
Suitable for freezing

Butter, *25g (1 oz)*
Onions, *2, chopped*
Vegetable stock cubes, *2, dissolved in 450ml (¾ pint) hot water*
Low-fat soft cheese, *200g (7oz)*
Fresh chives or parsley, *2 tablespoons, chopped + extra, for garnish*
Milk, *450ml (¾ pint)*
Cornflour, *2 level tablespoons, blended with a little milk*
French bread, *4 slices (not too thick)*
Garlic clove, *1, crushed*
Mature Cheddar cheese, *75g (3oz), finely grated*
Salt and freshly ground black pepper

This is the soup that's absolutely perfect for a cold winter's day. Piping hot, creamy and full of flavour, it's the ideal antidote to damp, chilly weather. The ingredients are inexpensive – and there's a fair chance of having them to hand at any time.

Just a couple of tips will guarantee this soup goes down a treat. Firstly, use good quality stock cubes and fresh herbs for the best flavour. Next, make sure that the Cheddar is very finely grated so that when you add it to the soup, it melts quickly. Lastly, don't boil the soup once the Cheddar has been added, or else the cheese could go stringy. You could use a tasty Lancashire cheese instead of Cheddar – just crumble it before you add it.

1 Melt half the butter in a large, heavy-based saucepan and add the onions. Cook them gently over a medium heat for a moment or two, give them a good stir, then put the lid on and allow them to 'sweat' over a very low heat for 3–4 minutes, without browning.

2 Pour in the vegetable stock, turn up the heat, and bring it to the boil. Reduce the heat and simmer, partially covered, for 10–15 minutes to cook the onions.

3 Transfer the mixture to a blender or food processor and add the soft cheese and chives or parsley. Blend for about 15–20 seconds, until smooth.

4 Return the soup to the saucepan and add the milk. Stir the blended cornflour mixture to make sure that it is smooth, then add it to the saucepan. Heat, stirring constantly until the soup thickens, then cook gently for 2–3 minutes over a low heat. This makes sure that the cornflour is properly cooked.

5 Meanwhile, make the garlic toasts. Grill the pieces of French bread on one side only, then spread the untoasted side with the remaining butter and the crushed garlic clove. Sprinkle about half the quantity of grated cheese evenly over the slices, then grill until bubbling and golden brown.

6 Just before serving the soup, remove the saucepan from the heat and sprinkle in the remaining Cheddar cheese, a little at a time, stirring as you go. Taste the soup and check the seasoning, adding salt and pepper as necessary.

7 Ladle the soup into warmed serving bowls and top each portion with a garlic cheese toast and some chopped chives or parsley.

COOK'S TIP:

▦ Another time, make the soup with 2 large leeks instead of the onions.

CREAMY RED PEPPER AND BUTTERNUT SQUASH SOUP

Butternut squash is readily available these days – so do try this smooth, thick soup with its amazing colour and flavour. It's easy to prepare, and it combines brilliantly with red peppers. Top the soup with a dollop of cream cheese and snipped fresh chives for a finishing touch.

SERVES 4

Suitable for vegetarians • Suitable for freezing

Butter, *25g (1oz)*

Onion, *1 large, chopped*

Butternut squash, *1 medium, peeled, deseeded and chopped into chunks*

Red pepper, *1, deseeded and chopped*

Vegetable stock cubes, *2, dissolved in 450ml (¾ pint) hot water*

Cream cheese, *200g (7oz)*

Milk, *450ml (¾ pint)*

Chives, *2 tablespoons, chopped*

Salt and freshly ground black pepper

1 Melt the butter in a very large saucepan. Add the onion and fry it gently for about 3 minutes, until softened, but not browned.

2 Add the butternut squash, red pepper and vegetable stock. Heat until the mixture is just simmering, then turn the heat to low and cook gently for about 20 minutes, partially covered, until the vegetables are soft and tender.

3 Transfer the mixture to a blender or food processor and add about half the cream cheese. Blend together for about 15–20 seconds, until completely smooth.

4 Return the mixture to the saucepan and add the milk and half the chives. Stir thoroughly and reheat until piping hot. Taste and adjust the seasoning.

5 Ladle the soup into warmed bowls, then top each portion with a dollop of the reserved cream cheese. Sprinkle with the remaining chives and a little extra ground black pepper, then serve.

COOK'S TIPS:

▨ If you're uncertain about how much butternut squash to use – as they do vary in size – you'll need roughly 500g (1lb 2oz) when peeled and deseeded. If you have any left over, simply boil it until tender to serve as a vegetable with another meal.

▨ The red pepper adds a delicious flavour to the soup, but if you're not keen on peppers, leave it out. The soup will still taste wonderful.

▨ If you don't want to serve all the soup at once, cool the remainder quickly, then refrigerate it for up to 3 days, or freeze it for up to 3 months.

AUTUMN VEGETABLE SOUP

A creamy vegetable soup that is economical and extremely good for you – it's just bursting with deliciously fresh flavours.

SERVES 6

Suitable for vegetarians • Suitable for freezing

Butter, *25g (1oz)*

Leek, *1, trimmed and sliced*

Onion, *1, chopped finely*

Courgette, *1, chopped*

Turnip, *225g (8oz), diced*

Carrot, *1 large, diced*

Potato, *1 medium, diced*

Vegetable stock cubes, *2, dissolved in 900ml (1½ pints) hot water*

Cornflour, *3 level tablespoons*

Milk, *600ml (1 pint)*

Sweetcorn, *75g (3oz)*

Single cream, *2–3 tablespoons*

Salt and freshly ground black pepper

Chopped fresh herbs, *to garnish*

1 Melt the butter in a large saucepan and sauté the leek, onion and courgette over a medium heat for 3–4 minutes until softened.
2 Next, add the turnip, carrot and potato. Cook, stirring often, for another 2–3 minutes.
3 Pour in the vegetable stock and increase the heat until just simmering, then reduce the heat and cook gently, with the lid on, for about 15–20 minutes, until the vegetables are tender.
4 Blend the cornflour to a smooth paste with 3–4 tablespoons of the milk. Add the remaining milk to the saucepan with the sweetcorn and single cream, then stir in the blended cornflour. Heat gently, stirring constantly until the soup thickens and just begins to boil. Cook for another 1–2 minutes over a very low heat.
5 Season to taste, then serve, garnished with chopped fresh herbs.

COOK'S TIP:

■ If you're following a low-fat diet, use skimmed milk and leave out the single cream – other guests can simply swirl some on the top of their bowlful.

CHUNKY HADDOCK AND PRAWN SOUP

You won't go hungry with a bowlful of this creamy, satisfying seafood soup. It's a meal in itself if you serve it with some fresh crusty bread and butter.

SERVES 4

Suitable for freezing

Butter, *25g (1oz)*

Spring onions, *1 bunch, trimmed and chopped*

Potato, *1 large, peeled and cut into chunks*

Vegetable stock cubes, *2, dissolved in 600ml (1 pint) water*

Smoked haddock or cod fillet, *350g (12oz), skinned and cut into chunks*

Milk, *450ml (¾ pint)*

Frozen peas, *50g (2oz)*

Peeled prawns, *50g (2oz)*

Parsley, *2 tablespoons, chopped*

Cornflour, *2 level tablespoons*

Salt and freshly ground black pepper

1 Melt the butter in a large saucepan. Add the spring onions and potato and cook gently, without browning, for 5 minutes.
2 Add the stock, bring up to the boil, then reduce the heat. Cover and simmer for about 10 minutes, until the potatoes are almost tender.
3 Add the fish, milk and peas. Heat and simmer gently until the fish is cooked – about 4 minutes. Next, add the prawns and half the parsley.
4 Blend the cornflour with 2–3 tablespoons of cold water. Add to the soup and cook gently, stirring all the time, until thickened. Cook gently for another minute or two, then taste and season.
5 Serve the soup in warmed bowls, garnished with the remaining parsley.

CHILLED FRESH HERB AND SOFT CHEESE SOUP

This soup is delicious if you serve it icy cold in summer, though it's just as tasty if you prefer your soups to be piping hot.

SERVES 4

Suitable for vegetarians • Suitable for freezing

Butter, *25g (1oz)*

Spring onions, *1 bunch, trimmed and chopped*

Rocket, watercress or spinach, *110g (4oz)*

Parsley, basil or coriander, *a generous handful*

Vegetable stock cubes, *2, dissolved in 300ml (½ pint) hot water*

Low-fat soft cheese, *200g (7oz)*

Cornflour, *1 level tablespoon*

Milk, *450ml (¾ pint)*

Salt and freshly ground black pepper

Natural yogurt or crème fraîche, *4 tablespoons*

Sprigs of rocket, watercress or herbs, *to garnish*

COOK'S TIP:

▪ Remember that a cold soup only works if it is served when really well chilled. It's a good idea to tell your guests that it is a chilled soup – or else they'll be surprised when they taste it.

1 Melt the butter in a large saucepan and sauté the spring onions until softened, but not browned – about 3–5 minutes. Add the rocket, watercress or spinach and parsley, basil or coriander. Cook, stirring occasionally, until the leaves have wilted – about another 2 minutes.

2 Add the vegetable stock and bring up to the boil, then cover, reduce the heat and simmer for 10 minutes.

3 Transfer the soup to a liquidiser or food processor and add the soft cheese. Blend for about 15 seconds until smooth, then return to the saucepan.

4 Blend the cornflour with 3–4 tablespoons of the milk, then stir into the soup. Bring up to the boil, stirring constantly, until thickened and smooth. Cook gently for another minute or so. The soup will be quite thick and concentrated at this stage.

5 Remove from the heat and gradually add the remaining milk, stirring well to keep the soup smooth. Transfer to a large bowl, then cover and chill until icy cold.

6 Taste and season the soup, then serve in chilled bowls, topped with natural yogurt or crème fraîche and garnished with sprigs of rocket, watercress or fresh herbs.

CHICKEN AND LEEK SOUP

In this recipe, you simmer a chicken quarter or chicken leg with the vegetables to give the soup a great flavour. It's inexpensive and very nourishing too.

SERVES 4

Suitable for freezing

Butter, *25g (1oz)*

Onion, *1 large, sliced*

Leeks, *2, sliced*

Chicken quarter or leg, *1*

Chicken stock cube, *1*

Bay leaves, *2*

Thyme leaves, *2 teaspoons(or 1 teaspoon dried)*

Small pasta shapes or long grain rice, *45g (1½oz)*

Parsley, *2 tablespoons, chopped*

Milk, *300ml (½ pint)*

Cornflour, *2 level tablespoons, blended with a little milk*

Salt and freshly ground black pepper

Thyme sprigs, *to garnish*

1   Melt the butter in a large saucepan. Add the onion and leeks and sauté them for about 3 minutes, until softened.

2   Add the chicken portion to the saucepan and pour in 900ml (1½ pints) of cold water. Add the stock cube, bay leaves and thyme. Bring up to the boil, then reduce the heat and simmer gently, partially covered, for about 45 minutes, until the chicken is very tender.

3   Lift the chicken portion from the saucepan and drain on kitchen paper. Allow it to cool for a few minutes.

4   Meanwhile, add the pasta shapes or rice to the saucepan and cook until tender. This will be about 5 minutes for small pasta shapes and 12 minutes for rice, though do check the pack instructions.

5   Whilst the pasta or rice is cooking, discard the skin and bones from the chicken, then use two forks to pull the meat apart into shreds – it will be very tender.

6   When the pasta or rice is cooked, add the parsley, milk and blended cornflour to the saucepan. Heat, stirring all the time, until the soup thickens. Add the shredded chicken to the saucepan, then cook gently for 1–2 minutes. Remove the bay leaves and season to taste, then serve the soup in warmed bowls, garnished with thyme sprigs.

COOK'S TIP:

■ For a more traditional cock-a-leekie soup, add 25g (1oz) of pearl barley when you first add the chicken, leave out the pasta or rice and substitute water for the milk. There's no need to thicken the soup if you prefer not to.

ALMOND AND LEMON SOUP

Don't be put off by the rather unusual idea of this soup – it is absolutely delicious.

SERVES 6

Suitable for vegetarians • Suitable for freezing

Butter, *40g (1½oz)*

Onion, *1, chopped*

Celery sticks, *3, chopped*

Vegetable stock cubes, *2, dissolved in 900ml (1½ pints) hot water*

Lemons, *2, finely grated zest and juice*

Bay leaves, *2*

Thyme leaves, *1 teaspoon (or ½ teaspoon of dried)*

Cornflour, *2 level tablespoons*

Milk, *300ml (½ pint)*

Ground almonds, *50g (2oz)*

Salt and freshly ground black pepper

Soured cream, single cream or crème fraîche, *6 tablespoons*

Flaked almonds, *25g (1oz), toasted*

Fresh thyme sprigs, *to garnish (optional)*

1   Melt the butter in a large saucepan and add the onion and celery. Sauté them gently for about 5 minutes, until softened, but not browned.
2   Add the stock, half the lemon zest and all the lemon juice. Pop the bay leaves and thyme into the saucepan. Bring up to the boil, then cover, reduce the heat and simmer gently for about 20 minutes.
3   Remove the bay leaves from the soup, then transfer it to a liquidiser or food processor and blend until smooth. Return to the saucepan.
4   Blend the cornflour with about 3–4 tablespoons of the milk, then stir into the soup with the remaining milk and ground almonds. Heat gently, stirring constantly, until thickened and smooth. Cook gently for another minute or two. Taste, adding salt and pepper to season.
5   Serve the soup in warmed bowls, topping each portion with a tablespoon of soured cream, single cream or crème fraîche, a few toasted flaked almonds and a little lemon zest. Garnish with sprigs of fresh thyme, if wished.

FLUFFY BAKED JACKETS WITH CHEESE AND CHIVES

Simple to make and utterly delicious to eat, you must make these potatoes to appreciate just how tasty they are.

SERVES 4

Suitable for vegetarians

Baking potatoes, *4 large*

Garlic and herb soft cheese, *1 x 125g (4½oz) tub*

Cheddar cheese, *50g (2oz), grated*

Tomatoes, *2 medium, chopped*

Fresh chives, *2 tablespoons, chopped*

Salt and freshly ground black pepper

Butter, *25g (1oz), to serve*

1   Preheat the oven to 200°C/400°F/Gas 6.
2   Prick the potatoes with a fork, then bake for about 1¼ hours, or until tender. Cool for a few minutes.
3   Halve the potatoes and scoop the flesh into a bowl, leaving the skins intact. Mash the potato flesh, then add the soft cheese, Cheddar, tomatoes and chives. Season with salt and pepper, then mix together.
4   Pile the mixture back into the potato skins. Place on a baking sheet, then return to the oven to heat through for about 15–20 minutes.
5   Serve, topped with a knob of butter.

COOK'S TIP:

■ If you can't get hold of any chives, use a couple of finely chopped spring onions instead.

CHEESE AND HERB PÂTÉ

This delicious cheese pâté can be put together in moments, and it's so versatile. Serve it as a starter or light meal with a fresh green salad and tomatoes, try spreading it onto Melba toast or crispbread, or use it as a toast topper and grill until bubbling. If you thin it down with natural yogurt, you can even use it as a dip for vegetable crudités.

MAKES ABOUT 6 SERVINGS

Suitable for vegetarians • Suitable for freezing

Cream cheese, *200g (7oz)*

Cheddar cheese, *110g (4oz), finely grated*

Red Leicester cheese, *75g (3oz), finely grated*

Spring onions, *2, trimmed and very finely chopped*

Parsley, *2 tablespoons, finely chopped*

Freshly ground black pepper

Milk, *2–3 tablespoons*

1 Put the cream cheese into a mixing bowl and beat it with a wooden spoon for a few moments to soften it.

2 Add the Cheddar and Red Leicester cheeses to the bowl with the spring onions and parsley. Season with black pepper – you do not need any salt – then work together to make a stiff paste, adding a little milk if necessary.

3 Spoon the pâté into a serving dish, then cover and refrigerate until ready to use.

COOK'S TIPS:

▓ For the best results, you must make sure that the cheeses are very finely grated.

▓ To transform this pâté into a delicious dip for fresh vegetable crudités, add 275g (10oz) of natural yogurt (two small pots) and mix in thoroughly.

TUNA AND RED LEICESTER PÂTÉ

A quick, easy and nutritious recipe that is also very, very tasty. It's brilliant served with home-made Melba toast, so here are the tricks to making it properly.

MAKES 6 SERVINGS

Suitable for freezing

Tuna in oil or brine, *1 x 200g (7oz) can, drained*

Red Leicester cheese, *200g (7oz) finely grated*

Natural yogurt, *150g (5oz)*

Lemon zest, *1 teaspoon, finely grated*

Lemon juice, *1 teaspoon*

Parsley or chives, *1 tablespoon, chopped*

Freshly ground black pepper

Medium sliced white bread, *6 slices, from a large loaf*

1 Tip the drained tuna into a mixing bowl and add the cheese, yogurt, lemon zest, lemon juice and parsley or chives. Season with a few good turns from the pepper grinder. You're unlikely to need any salt, though add a little if you wish.

2 Mix all the ingredients together until just combined – you want to retain some texture, so avoid over-mixing. Cover and chill until ready to eat.

3 To make the Melba toast, grill the slices of bread on both sides. Cut the crusts off at this stage. Next, use a bread knife to cut through the middle of each slice of bread to create two very thin slices. This is much easier than it sounds! Slice these pieces diagonally in half, then grill the untoasted sides until light golden brown.

COOK'S TIP:

▓ Keep an eye on the Melba toast when it is under the grill, as the pieces will curl up and could burn.

WARM MEDITERRANEAN POTATO SALAD

This potato salad tastes superb with its mix of Mediterranean flavours. Try it as a light meal by itself or with other salads, or serve with grilled fish or cold, cooked meats. It's excellent as part of a buffet spread too.

SERVES 4

Suitable for vegetarians

New potatoes, *675g (1½ lb)*

Butter, *25g (1oz)*

Red pepper, *1 small, deseeded and sliced*

Yellow pepper, *1 small, deseeded and sliced*

Sun-dried tomato paste, *3 tablespoons*

Lemon juice, *2 tablespoons*

Cherry tomatoes, *110g (4oz)*

Somerset brie, *110g (4oz), cut into small cubes*

Black and green olives, *50g (2oz)*

Salt and freshly ground black pepper

Basil leaves, *about a dozen*

1   Scrub the potatoes, then put them into a saucepan with just enough water to cover. Add a pinch of salt. Bring to the boil, then cover, reduce the heat and simmer gently until just tender – about 15 minutes.

2   Meanwhile, melt the butter in a frying pan and sauté the peppers until very soft – about 6–8 minutes. Do this over a medium-low heat so that they don't go brown.

3   Mix together the sun-dried tomato paste and lemon juice in a large mixing bowl. Drain the cooked potatoes and add to the bowl with the peppers and the buttery pan juices, tossing everything together gently until coated.

4   When the potatoes have cooled for a few minutes, add the tomatoes, Somerset brie and olives, stirring gently to mix. Season to taste with salt and pepper, then serve, scattered with the basil leaves.

COOK'S TIPS:

▧ Adding the hot potatoes to the dressing means that they absorb the flavours as they cool down.

▧ You could substitute tomato purée for the sun-dried tomato paste, and look out for bottled roast peppers to use instead of fresh ones. If you're not fond of olives, simply leave them out.

BACON, EGG AND POTATO SAUTÉ

A quick and easy recipe that makes the most of some simple ingredients, transforming them into a mouth-watering dish for breakfast or brunch. And it's perfect when you want a quick filler at any time of the day.

SERVES 2

Butter, *15g (½ oz)*

Olive oil, *2 teaspoons*

Streaky bacon, *4 rashers, chopped*

Cold, cooked potatoes, *350g (12oz), cut into chunks*

Spring onions, *4, trimmed and chopped*

Eggs, *2*

Paprika, *large pinch*

Salt and freshly ground black pepper

1   Heat the butter and olive oil in a frying pan and add the bacon. Cook for about 2 minutes, stirring often. Add the potatoes and sauté them for about 5–6 minutes until they are golden. Stir in the spring onions and cook for another minute or two.

2   Make two spaces in the middle of the frying pan and crack an egg into each space. Cook gently until the eggs are set – about 5–6 minutes. Sprinkle with the paprika and season with salt and pepper. Serve at once.

COOK'S TIP:

▧ If you like, add three or four sliced mushrooms or a chopped red pepper to the frying pan with the potatoes.

CHEESE AND HAM GRATINS

Gratins such as these taste so good, and they're very simple to make. They're perfect for a light meal with salad and crusty bread, or if you want to serve them as starters, halve the quantities and use small gratin dishes.

SERVES 4

Butter, *50g (2oz), softened*
Dry mustard powder or English mustard, *1 teaspoon*
Spinach, *175g (6oz)*
Cheddar cheese, *110g (4oz), grated*
Cooked ham, *8 small slices*
Fresh breadcrumbs, *4 tablespoons*
Single cream, *150ml (¼ pint)*
Salt and freshly ground black pepper

1 Put the softened butter into a bowl with the mustard powder or English mustard and mix together thoroughly. Use half this mixture to butter four individual gratin dishes or shallow heatproof dishes.

2 Wash the spinach and pack it into a saucepan. Cook it for about 2–3 minutes, without adding any water to the saucepan, until the leaves have wilted. Drain well, squeezing out the excess moisture with the back of a spoon.

3 Sprinkle a little of the cheese into the base of each dish. Arrange two slices of ham in each dish

with an equal amount of spinach. Sprinkle the remaining cheese and breadcrumbs evenly over the surface.

4 Pour an equal amount of cream into each dish, then season with a little pepper. Dot the surface with the remaining butter mixture.

5 Preheat the grill. Pop the dishes under the grill and cook until the cheese bubbles and turns golden brown. This will take about 3–4 minutes. Do keep an eye on them to make sure that they don't burn. Serve at once.

COOK'S TIPS:

▓ If you're not keen on mustard, add ½ teaspoon of finely grated lemon zest or 1 tablespoon of chopped fresh parsley to the butter instead.

▓ You could bake these dishes in the oven, if you prefer. They will require about 10–12 minutes at 190°C/375°F/ Gas 5.

▓ Assemble these dishes ahead of time, if you like, up to the point before cooking. Cover and refrigerate until you need them, then bake in the oven to make sure that they are thoroughly hot.

SOMERSET BRIE ON HOT FRENCH BREAD

This tasty snack for two can be made in a matter of minutes. It's mouthwatering and moreish, so if you're very hungry, double the quantities.

SERVES 2

Suitable for vegetarians

Butter, *25g (1oz)*

Shallots, *about 8, halved*

Garlic clove, *1, thinly sliced*

Pepper, *1 yellow or red, halved and deseeded*

French stick, *1 generous piece, sliced in half*

Somerset brie, *110g (4oz), sliced into 2 wedges*

1 Melt the butter in a frying pan and add the shallots and garlic, cooking them over a low heat until browned and crispy.

2 Meanwhile, grill the pepper halves until beginning to char, turning them over once.

3 Push the shallots and garlic to one side of the frying pan, then put in the French bread, cut side down. Let it brown for a few minutes, then put the pieces on to heat-resistant serving plates.

4 Top the bread with the shallots, garlic and pepper halves, then with a wedge of Somerset brie. Grill for a few moments until it begins to melt, then serve immediately.

COOK'S TIP:

▪ Use your favourite British cheese in this recipe – a good slice of Derbyshire, Cheshire or Lancashire would be wonderful, and if you're a blue cheese fan, then Stilton is the one for you.

BUBBLING WELSH RAREBITS WITH CRISPY BACON

There's nothing like the smell of sizzling bacon and bubbling cheese to make your mouth water, so combine the two in this scrumptious snack.

SERVES 6

Butter, *50g (2oz)*

Dry mustard powder, *1 teaspoon*

Cayenne pepper, *good pinch*

Worcestershire sauce, *a few drops*

Caerphilly cheese, *175g (6oz), grated*

Streaky bacon, *6 rashers*

French bread, *1 stick, sliced*

Cherry tomatoes, *about 12*

1 In a bowl, beat the butter with a wooden spoon until it has softened. Add the mustard powder, cayenne pepper and Worcestershire sauce and beat again until smooth. Add the cheese and work together until combined.

2 Preheat the grill. Arrange the bacon rashers on the grill rack and cook until crispy. Set to one side.

3 Toast the French bread on one side only. Spread the cheese mixture on the untoasted side, then arrange on the grill rack with the cherry tomatoes. Grill until the cheese melts and bubbles.

4 Serve the Welsh rarebits whilst piping hot, topped with the bacon rashers and garnished with the grilled cherry tomatoes.

COOK'S TIPS:

■ Instead of Worcestershire sauce, why not try using mushroom ketchup? It has a very similar consistency, and gives a tasty kick to the cheese mixture.

■ You don't have to use French bread – any crusty loaf will work well.

■ Try tasty Lancashire or creamy Double Gloucester cheese instead of Caerphilly, for a change.

chicken and turkey

From a fabulous butter-roast chicken to the most amazing casseroles, sautés and stir-fries, you'll find recipes in this chapter to really satisfy your passion for poultry – and expand your repertoire of favourites. Whether you are searching for a recipe for a speedy family supper, or you want to try something different for a special occasion, you're sure to find a recipe that's just what you're looking for.

Most of us are happy to experiment with new flavours these days, and there are many influences from overseas within these pages. You might fancy Italian-style Chicken in White Wine, or how about Thai Red Chicken Curry? Then there's a fabulous recipe for Chicken Marinated in Yogurt and Indian Spices, or do you feel like a good old-fashioned Puff-topped Turkey Pie? No problem – there's a recipe here to suit you.

Getting the hang of...

Roasting a chicken couldn't be easier – you just whack it in the oven and wait. Yet what if you've never roasted a bird in your life before? How do you judge when it's properly cooked? This recipe will help you get the hang of roasting a chicken to perfection. And if you've roasted half a million birds before, try this method for producing succulent, tender results.

Just a couple of things to bear in mind that are really important. When you buy your chicken, keep it cool and away from other foods and bring it home as quickly as possible. Refrigerate at once, keeping it at the bottom of the fridge – the coolest part – loosely wrapped in greaseproof paper, foil or cling film. Cook within a day or two of buying, and make sure that the bird is thoroughly cooked before you serve it – following the recipe here.

BUTTER-ROAST CHICKEN WITH GARLIC

Roasting a chicken in this way – smothered with butter and wrapped in greaseproof paper to trap all the wonderful juices – keeps it moist and full of flavour.

SERVES 2, 4 OR 6

Chicken, *1, small, medium or large*

Lemon, *1*

Butter, *50g (2oz), softened*

Salt and freshly ground black pepper

Thyme or rosemary sprigs, *about 6*

Garlic cloves, *12*

1 Preheat the oven to 190°C/375°F/Gas 5. Calculate the cooking time for the size of chicken that you have bought. It will require 20 minutes per 450g (1lb), plus a further 20 minutes, so a 1.8kg (4lb) bird will take 1 hour 40 minutes to roast.
2 Take a very large sheet of greaseproof paper, big enough to wrap around the chicken, with plenty of extra room for folding it over.
3 Put the chicken onto the middle of the paper, then push half a lemon into the body cavity of the bird to give it a lovely lemony flavour as it cooks.

4 Smear the butter all over the chicken with your hands, then season with salt and freshly ground black pepper. Slice the remaining lemon and place on top of the chicken with the thyme or rosemary sprigs. Scatter the garlic around the bird, then wrap with the greaseproof paper, folding it to make a loose parcel. Lift into a baking dish or roasting tin.
5 Roast the chicken for the calculated time. Check that the bird is thoroughly cooked by piercing the thickest part of the thigh with a sharp knife or skewer. If the juices run clear, and there is no trace of pink, the chicken is cooked. If the juices are still slightly pink, roast for another 10 minutes or until done. Leave to rest for 5–10 minutes, then unwrap, carve and serve with the softened garlic cloves.

COOK'S TIP:

■ Roast garlic has a much sweeter, milder flavour than you might imagine, though you could use about 8 shallots, if you prefer.

ITALIAN-STYLE CHICKEN IN WHITE WINE

There may be rather a long list of ingredients for this recipe, but don't let that put you off, as this dish is very easy to make – and the results are simply wonderful.

SERVES 4

Suitable for freezing

Butter, *25g (1oz)*

Streaky bacon, *50g (2oz), snipped into small pieces*

Chicken quarters, *4*

Plain flour, *2 level tablespoons*

Onion, *1, thickly sliced*

Garlic cloves, *1–2, finely sliced*

Red or green pepper, *1, deseeded and sliced*

Carrot, *1, thinly sliced*

Courgette, *1, halved and sliced*

Button mushrooms, *175g (6oz)*

Tomatoes, *4, quartered*

Chicken stock cube, *1, dissolved in 150ml (¼ pint) hot water*

White wine, *150ml (¼ pint)*

Tomato purée, *1 tablespoon*

Green and black olives, *about 16*

Basil leaves, *about a dozen + extra for garnish*

Salt and freshly ground black pepper

1 Melt the butter in a large flameproof casserole dish or deep-sided sauté pan and add the streaky bacon. Cook gently for about 3–4 minutes.

2 Meanwhile, dust the chicken portions with the flour, then add to the cooking pot and fry until well-browned on both sides. Remove the chicken and set to one side whilst frying the vegetables.

3 Sauté the onion, garlic and pepper for about 3 minutes, until softened. Add the carrot, courgette, mushrooms, tomatoes, stock, wine, tomato purée, olives and basil, stirring to mix. Return the chicken portions, heat until simmering point, then cover and cook over a low heat for about 1 hour.

4 Remove the lid and cook for another few minutes to reduce the liquid slightly. Test that the chicken is thoroughly cooked by piercing the thickest part with a sharp knife – there shouldn't be any trace of pink juices. If there are, cook for a little longer.

5 Taste and season, then serve with pasta or potatoes. Garnish with lots of fresh basil leaves – be generous!

COOK'S TIPS:

▒ Stir a big knob of butter through the pasta before you serve to give a delicious flavour.

▒ The olives will mellow during cooking, but if you really don't like them, leave them out. The same goes for the pepper too.

CHICKEN, PESTO AND BASIL PARCELS

This special chicken recipe is easy to make – and tastes spectacular.

SERVES 4

Suitable for freezing

Fresh breadcrumbs, *2 tablespoons*

Red or green pesto sauce, *2 tablespoons*

Mature Cheddar cheese, *25g (1oz), finely grated*

Boneless chicken breasts, *4*

Basil leaves, *about 20, plus extra, to garnish*

Salt and freshly ground black pepper

Red or yellow peppers, *2, deseeded and quartered*

Tomatoes, *4, cut into wedges*

Olive oil, *2 tablespoons*

Butter, *15g (½oz)*

1 Preheat the oven to 200°C/400°F/Gas 6.

2 Mix together the breadcrumbs, pesto sauce and Cheddar cheese.

3 Using a sharp knife, cut a pocket into each chicken breast. Fill each pocket with about 5 basil leaves and an equal amount of the cheese and pesto mixture. Season with salt and pepper, then close the pocket and secure with cocktail sticks or skewers.

4 Put the peppers and tomatoes into a roasting dish or baking dish and arrange the chicken breasts on top. Drizzle with the olive oil and dot with the butter.

5 Roast for about 25 minutes until the chicken is thoroughly cooked. Check with a sharp knife – the juices should run clear. Serve, garnished with basil leaves.

COOK'S TIP:

▓ Instead of pesto sauce, try sun-dried tomato paste. It has a deliciously intense flavour and works well in this recipe.

LEMON CHICKEN WITH GARLIC AND ROSEMARY

Rosemary, lemon and garlic taste so good together in this easy chicken dish.

SERVES 4

Butter, *50g (2oz)*

Olive oil, *1 tablespoon*

Boneless chicken breasts, *4*

Red or Spanish onion, *1, sliced*

Lemons, *2, scrubbed*

Rosemary sprigs, *a few + extra for garnish*

Garlic cloves, *8, peeled*

Crème fraîche or soured cream, *150g (5oz)*

Salt and freshly ground black pepper

1 Heat the butter and olive oil in a large frying pan and add the chicken breasts and onion. Cook over a medium heat for 8–10 minutes, turning the chicken occasionally.

2 Squeeze the juice from one lemon and add to the frying pan with the rosemary and garlic cloves and cook over a low heat for 15–20 minutes, until the chicken is tender and thoroughly cooked. Check with a sharp knife inserted into the thickest part – there should be no trace of pink juices. If there are, cook for a little longer.

3 Add the crème fraîche or soured cream to the chicken, stirring it through until incorporated. Check the seasoning, then serve the chicken, garnished with lemon zest, lemon wedges and rosemary sprigs.

COOK'S TIP:

■ Garlic cloves have a milder flavour when cooked whole, so don't be put off by the quantity.

CHICKEN, CELERY AND APRICOT SAUTÉ

Tasty, satisfying and a cinch to make – you'll enjoy this aromatic chicken dish.

SERVES 6

Suitable for freezing

Chicken breasts, *6*

Plain flour, *2 level tablespoons*

Salt and freshly ground black pepper

Olive oil, *2 tablespoons*

Butter, *25g (1oz)*

Onion, *1, chopped*

Celery, *3 sticks, chopped*

Ready-to-eat dried apricots, *75g (3oz), roughly chopped*

White wine, *150ml (¼ pint)*

Chicken stock cube, *1, dissolved in 150ml (¼ pint) hot water*

Fresh herb sprigs
(e.g. rosemary, bay leaves or thyme)

1   Rinse the chicken breasts and pat dry with kitchen paper. Put the flour onto a plate, season with salt and pepper, then use to lightly coat the chicken.

2   Heat the olive oil and butter in a deep frying pan or flameproof casserole. Add the chicken breasts and cook them for about 10 minutes, turning occasionally, until well browned.

3   Add the onion, celery and apricots and cook for a few minutes. Pour in the white wine and stock and add the fresh herb sprigs. Bring up to the boil, then reduce the heat and simmer for about 30 minutes, partially covered, until the chicken is tender.

4   To test the chicken, pierce the thickest part with a sharp knife – the juices should run clear. If they still look slightly pink, cook for another few minutes.

5   Remove the herb sprigs. Serve the chicken with potatoes or rice and seasonal vegetables, such as cabbage or broccoli.

COOK'S TIP:

▥   Use a dry white wine for this recipe, though it doesn't have to be an expensive one. If you like olives, add a few with the wine and stock.

CHICKEN MARINATED IN YOGURT AND INDIAN SPICES

This chicken is so moist and full of flavour – you'll love it. It's a perfect recipe for the summer months, when you can prepare the food ahead, ready for barbecuing or grilling later in the day.

SERVES 4

Suitable for freezing

Skinless, boneless chicken breasts, *4*

White or white wine vinegar, *150ml (¼ pint)*

Salt, *2 teaspoons*

Garlic cloves, *2, finely chopped*

Chilli powder, *2 level teaspoons*

Root ginger, *2 teaspoons, peeled and grated*

Fresh coriander or mint sprigs, *a few, chopped*

Cumin seeds or ground cumin, *1 teaspoon*

Natural yogurt, *150g (5oz)*

Onion slices, garlic and lemon wedges, *to garnish*

1   Rinse the chicken breasts and put them into a bowl. Add the vinegar and salt, stir, then cover and refrigerate for 30–35 minutes, but no longer.

2   Meanwhile mix together all the remaining ingredients to make the marinade – do this in a blender if you like.

3   Drain the chicken really well, discarding the vinegar. Add the chicken to the marinade, stirring to coat. Cover and refrigerate for 3–4 hours, or overnight.

4   Cook the chicken on the barbecue or under a medium-hot grill for about 20–25 minutes, turning once and basting with the marinade. Add the onion slices, garlic and lemon wedges to the grill pan for the final few minutes.

5   To check that the chicken is thoroughly cooked, pierce the thickest part with a knife – there shouldn't be any trace of pink juices. If there are, cook for a few more minutes.

COOK'S TIP:

▓ You could chop the chicken into large chunks and thread onto soaked wooden kebab sticks or skewers – the cooking time will be reduced by a few minutes. Serve stuffed into warmed pitta bread, with salad.

POUSSIN WITH ORANGE AND SPICES

Poussin are simply small chickens, about 4–6 weeks old, and small ones are perfect for a single serving. They taste best when cooked with lots of flavour – like they are here.

SERVES 4

Butter, *50g (2oz)*

Poussin, *4 small*

Shallots, *8, halved*

Oranges, *2 small, cut into wedges*

Cumin seeds, *1 teaspoon*

Coriander seeds, *1 teaspoon, lightly crushed*

Green or black olives, *12 large*

Salt and freshly ground black pepper

Fresh coriander sprigs, *to garnish*

1   Preheat the oven to 190°C/375°F/Gas 5. Melt the butter and use some of it to brush the inside of a roasting tin or baking dish large enough to hold the poussin.

2   Put the poussin into the baking dish, brush liberally with melted butter, then add the shallots and chunks of orange. Sprinkle with the cumin and coriander seeds, add the olives, then season with salt and black pepper.

3   Transfer the roasting tin or dish to the oven and roast for 1 hour, basting from time to time. To make sure that the birds are thoroughly cooked, test the thickest part with a sharp knife – the juices should run clear. If not, roast for another 5–10 minutes.

4   Serve the poussin with the shallots and orange wedges, garnished with fresh coriander sprigs.

COOK'S TIP:

▓ The weight of poussin ranges from about 350–600g (12oz–1lb 5oz), so choose the smaller ones for single servings. If you prefer, use two small chickens, halved.

THAI RED CHICKEN CURRY

A mild Thai curry that's a real winner – and it's so quick and easy to make. Ingredients are readily available, and some of them are partially prepared, making it effortless to put together.

SERVES 4

Suitable for freezing

Butter, *40g (1½oz)*

Shallots, *6, peeled and sliced*

Garlic cloves, *2, crushed*

Skinless, boneless chicken breasts, *4, sliced into thick strips*

Lemon grass, *1 tablespoon ready-prepared "fresh"*

Root ginger, *2 teaspoons, peeled and grated (or use ready-prepared)*

Coconut milk, *1 x 400ml can*

Chicken stock cube, *1, dissolved in 150ml (¼ pint) hot water*

Thai red curry paste, *3 – 4 teaspoons*

Fish sauce or light soy sauce, *2 tablespoons*

Fresh coriander or basil, *2 tablespoons, chopped*

Salt and freshly ground black pepper

Single cream, *4 tablespoons*

1 Melt the butter in a wok or large frying pan. Add the shallots, garlic and chicken and sauté over a medium-high heat for about 4–5 minutes, or until the chicken is sealed and browned.

2 Add the lemon grass, ginger, coconut milk, chicken stock and red curry paste. Stir in the fish sauce or soy sauce and coriander or basil. Bring up to the boil, then reduce the heat and simmer for 20–25 minutes, until the chicken is cooked and the sauce has reduced a little.

3 Taste the chicken curry, seasoning with salt and pepper, if necessary. Stir in the single cream, then serve, accompanied by rice or noodles.

COOK'S TIP:

▥ Buy prepared lemon grass, root ginger, "fresh" coriander and Thai red curry paste in small jars from supermarkets and delicatessen – just look in the oriental food section. Keep them in the refrigerator once opened.

STILTON-STUFFED CHICKEN BREASTS

Perfect for a dinner party or celebration meal, this is a wonderful way to transform chicken breasts into a really special dish.

SERVES 4

Butter, *50g (2oz), softened*

Blue Stilton, *50g (2oz)*

Skinless, boneless chicken breasts, *4 large*

Salt and freshly ground black pepper

Streaky bacon, *8 rashers, de-rinded*

Olive oil, *1 tablespoon*

Chicken stock cubes, *2, dissolved in 200ml (⅓ pint) hot water*

Red wine, *450ml (¾ pint)*

1 Reserve 15g (½oz) of the butter and put the rest into a small bowl with the Stilton. Mix together to make a stiff paste, then chill for 10 minutes.

2 Meanwhile, flatten the chicken breasts by placing them between sheets of cling film or greaseproof paper and beating them with a wooden meat mallet or rolling pin. Do this evenly so that they don't fall apart.

3 Roll the cheese mixture into 4 cylinder shapes and put one onto each chicken breast. Season, then roll up to make a neat parcel. Wrap each one with 2 bacon rashers and secure them with cocktail sticks.

4 Heat the reserved butter with the oil in a large frying pan. Add the chicken and fry on all sides until well-browned. This will take about 10 minutes.

5 Pour in the stock and wine. Heat until simmering, then partially cover and cook for about 35 minutes, turning the chicken occasionally, and removing the lid for the last 15 minutes to allow the liquid to reduce down slightly.

COOK'S TIPS:

▪ Add a 10g pack of dried porcini mushrooms to the pan with the red wine for a delicious flavour.

▪ You could make this dish with white wine instead of red for a change.

ROAST CORN-FED CHICKEN WITH HERB BUTTER

Corn-fed chicken has a delicious flavour which this recipe enhances perfectly.

SERVES 4

Corn-fed chicken portions, *4*

Onion, *1 large, cut into wedges*

Butter, *50g (2oz), softened*

Tarragon, *1 tablespoon, chopped*

Parsley, *1 tablespoon, chopped*

Bay leaves, *about 4*

Salt and freshly ground black pepper

Brandy, *2 tablespoons*

Single cream, *150ml (¼ pint)*

Cornflour, *2 teaspoons, blended with 6 tablespoons cold water*

1   Preheat the oven to 190°C/375°F/Gas 5.

2   Arrange the chicken portions in a roasting pan and surround with the onion wedges.

3   Mix together the butter, chopped tarragon and parsley, then spread over the chicken. Add the bay leaves, then season with salt and pepper.

4   Roast the chicken for approximately 45 minutes, until cooked. Test that it is thoroughly done by piercing the thickest part with a sharp knife – the juices should run clear.

5   Lift the chicken portions onto warmed serving plates and keep warm whilst you quickly make the sauce.

6   Add the brandy to the pan juices and onions, then cook over a high heat on the hob for a few moments to burn off the alcohol. Remove the bay leaves. Stir in the cream and blended cornflour, then cook gently, stirring until thickened and smooth. Season to taste, then serve with the chicken.

COOK'S TIP:

■   If you can't find corn-fed chicken portions, just use ordinary ones instead.

TASTY TURKEY NOODLES

Try turkey stir-fry strips in a spicy sauce with red pepper, carrot, broccoli and instant noodles for a very tasty low-fat meal.

SERVES 4

Thread egg noodles, *175g (6oz)*

Chicken stock cube, *1, dissolved in 200ml (⅓ pint) water*

Crunchy peanut butter, *2 tablespoons*

Soy sauce, *2 tablespoons*

Sweet chilli sauce, *2–3 teaspoons, according to taste*

Cornflour, *2 teaspoons*

Butter, *40g (1½oz)*

Turkey stir-fry strips, *350g (12oz)*

Carrot, *1 large, cut into fine strips*

Red pepper, *1, deseeded and cut into fine strips*

Broccoli, *175g (6oz), broken into small florets*

Garlic cloves, *2, crushed*

Root ginger, *1 tablespoon, finely grated*

Fresh coriander, *1 tablespoon, chopped*

Sesame seeds and coriander sprigs, *to garnish*

1   Put the noodles into a bowl and cover with boiling water. Allow to soak for about 6 minutes, or according to pack instructions.

2   Mix together the chicken stock, peanut butter, soy sauce, chilli sauce and cornflour. Set to one side.

3   Melt the butter in a large frying pan or wok and add the turkey strips. Sauté for 3–4 minutes until browned, then add the carrot, pepper, broccoli, garlic, ginger and coriander. Sauté for a further 3–4 minutes.

4   Stir the stock mixture and add to the frying pan or wok with the drained noodles. Heat, stirring, for 2–3 minutes, then serve in warmed bowls, sprinkled with sesame seeds and garnished with sprigs of coriander.

COOK'S TIP:

▓ Look out for prepared "fresh" garlic and ginger in small jars. Keep in the fridge once opened, and use within 6 weeks.

TURKEY STEAKS WITH SPICED LEMON BUTTER

Fire up your tastebuds with this spicy little number – cooked on the barbecue, under the grill or in a griddle pan.

SERVES 4

Turkey steaks, *4, weighing about 175–225g (6–8oz) each*

Olive oil, *2 tablespoons*

Salt and freshly ground black pepper

Cajun seasoning, *2 teaspoons*

Butter, *25g (1oz)*

Lemon zest, *1 teaspoon, finely grated*

Lemon, *1, cut into wedges*

Natural yogurt, *150g (5oz)*

Cucumber or red pepper, *2 tablespoons, finely chopped*

Coriander or parsley, *1 tablespoon, chopped*

1   Preheat a barbecue, grill or griddle pan.
2   Brush the turkey steaks liberally with the olive oil and season with salt and pepper. Cook on the barbecue, under the grill or in the griddle pan for about 10–12 minutes, turning once.
3   Meanwhile, mix together the Cajun seasoning, butter and lemon zest.
4   Spread the flavoured butter over the turkey steaks and cook for another 3–4 minutes, adding the lemon wedges to brown them slightly. Check that the steaks are thoroughly cooked by piercing the thickest part with a sharp knife – the juices should run clear.
5   Mix together the yogurt, cucumber or pepper and coriander or parsley. Serve with the turkey steaks.

COOK'S TIP:

■   Use skinless, boneless chicken breasts, if you like. Flatten then slightly first with a meat mallet or rolling pin.

PUFF-TOPPED TURKEY PIE

Tuck into a plateful of this delicious turkey pie – topped with a ready-rolled puff pastry sheet for ease and speed.

SERVES 4

Suitable for freezing

Broccoli, *110g (4oz), broken into small florets*

Butter, *40g (1½oz)*

Bacon, *2 rashers, snipped into pieces*

Leek or onion, *1, sliced*

Plain flour, *40g (1½oz)*

Milk, *450ml (¾ pint)*

Mushrooms, *75g (3oz), wiped and sliced*

Cooked turkey, *350g (12oz), chopped*

Parsley, *1 tablespoon, chopped*

Salt and freshly ground black pepper

Ready-rolled puff pastry sheet, *1 x 375g (13oz), defrosted if frozen*

Beaten egg or milk, *to glaze*

1   Cook the broccoli in a small amount of lightly salted boiling water for 4–5 minutes. Drain thoroughly.

2   Meanwhile, melt the butter in a large saucepan and gently fry the bacon for 2 minutes. Add the leek or onion and cook gently for 3–4 minutes, until softened, but not browned.

3   Add the flour to the saucepan. Stir and cook gently over a low heat for 1 minute, then remove from the heat. Gradually add the milk, stirring well to mix it in. Return to the heat and bring to the boil, stirring constantly, until the sauce is smooth and thick.

4   Add the broccoli, mushrooms, turkey and parsley to the sauce, mixing together well. Season to taste.

5   Preheat the oven to 220°C/425°F/Gas 7. Lightly grease a 1.2 litre (2 pint) earthenware pie dish.

6   Unroll the pastry sheet, invert the pie dish on top, then cut around the edge to give you the lid. Use the pastry trimmings to cut out thin strips to lay around the rim of the dish. Cut out leaves from any remaining pastry for decoration.

7   Pour the filling into the pie dish. Lay the strips of pastry around the rim, brush with a little water, then fit the lid on top, pressing down well to seal. Cut a small hole in the centre of the pie to allow steam to escape. Decorate with pastry leaves, then flute the edge with a sharp knife. Brush the pastry with beaten egg or milk, to glaze.

8   Bake for 25–30 minutes until risen and golden brown.

COOK'S TIPS:

■   Puff pastry rises best when you cut the edges cleanly, so use a sharp knife.

■   Use cooked chicken instead of turkey, and vary the vegetables as you wish.

TURKEY, GRAPE AND CRUNCHY NUT SALAD

A refreshingly different way to serve turkey or chicken – with crisp lettuce, grapes, apples and crunchy butter-fried nuts.

SERVES 4

Butter, *50g (2oz)*

Vegetable oil, *1 tablespoon*

Hazelnuts, *25g (1oz)*

Flaked almonds, *25g (1oz)*

Cooked turkey or chicken, *350g (12oz), chopped into chunks*

Lemon juice, *2 tablespoons*

Apple, *1, chopped*

Seedless red or green grapes, *110g (4oz)*

Red onion, *½ small, finely sliced*

Mixed lettuce leaves, *1 large handful*

Salt and freshly ground black pepper

Cos or Romaine lettuce, *1*

Natural low-fat yogurt, *to serve (optional)*

1 Heat the butter and oil in a large frying pan or wok. Add the hazelnuts and almonds and cook them gently, stirring often, for about 2 minutes, until browned. Lift them out with a draining spoon onto sheets of kitchen paper.

2 Add the turkey or chicken chunks to the frying pan or wok and cook for 2–3 minutes, until browned and crispy. Drain on sheets of kitchen paper.

3 Put the lemon juice into a large bowl and add the apple, grapes, red onion and mixed lettuce leaves, tossing them together. Mix in the nuts and turkey or chicken and season with salt and pepper.

4 Arrange the cos or Romaine lettuce leaves in 4 salad bowls, then share out the turkey mixture between them. Drizzle with a little natural yogurt, if you like, then serve.

COOK'S TIPS:

▩ Whilst this is a perfect recipe for using up leftover turkey or chicken, you can also use fresh stir-fry strips, cooking them in the butter and oil for a few more minutes.

▩ No red onion? Use 4 or 5 chopped spring onions instead.

TURKEY TORTILLAS WITH SALSA AND GUACAMOLE

For a Mexican style meal, try cooked turkey or chicken wrapped in warm soft tortillas with a lively salsa, guacamole and fresh soured cream.

SERVES 4

Tomatoes, *4*

Cucumber, *10cm (4 inch) piece, finely chopped*

Red onion, *1 small, finely chopped*

Fresh coriander or mint, *2 tablespoons, chopped*

Lemon juice, *2 tablespoons*

Salt and freshly ground black pepper

Avocado, *1 large*

Soft tortillas, *8*

Cooked turkey, *350g (12oz), chopped*

Fresh soured cream, *150ml (¼ pint)*

Cheddar cheese, *75g (3oz), grated*

1 To make the salsa, chop 3 tomatoes finely, then mix with the cucumber, red onion and herbs. Add a couple of teaspoons of lemon juice and season with salt and pepper.

2 For the guacamole, skin the remaining tomato by covering it with boiling water for about 1 minute, then chop finely, removing the seeds. Halve the avocado and remove the stone, then scoop the flesh into a bowl and mash with a fork. Add the remaining lemon juice and chopped tomato. Season and stir well.

3 Warm the tortillas in a low oven or under a medium grill for about 5 minutes. Lay them on a work top and spoon on some salsa and cooked turkey. Top with the avocado mixture and soured cream, then fold over and serve, sprinkled with the grated cheese.

COOK'S TIP:

▮ If you prefer, use fresh turkey or chicken stir-fry strips, cooking them in a little butter and oil for about 10–12 minutes, until thoroughly cooked.

beef, lamb, pork and bacon

Doesn't the Peppered Fillet Steak with Mushrooms and Melting Stilton on page 51 simply make your mouth water? You can almost hear the steak sizzling in the pan. And imagine how good it tastes. Yet it's just one of fifteen fantastic recipes contained within these pages.

There's a really great selection of tasty food in this chapter – and it's not all for those occasions when you want something out of the ordinary. In fact, there's a good choice of family fillers, such as Minty Lamb Burgers with Mustard Dressing, or homely Beef Casserole with Horseradish and Parsley Dumplings. A special mention too for Lamb Cutlets with Roasted Winter Vegetables, and Savoury Bread and Butter Pudding with Ham, Leeks and Cheese – two exceptionally easy recipes that give marvellous results.

Getting the hang of...

YORKSHIRE PUDDING ROAST

What better way to serve a delicious roast dinner than in a golden, puffed-up Yorkshire pudding? This is a recipe all the family will love.

It's well worth getting to know how to make Yorkshire puddings properly, for they really are sensational with roast beef. In this recipe, four large puddings are made to act as nifty containers for the roast dinner, but you don't have to make them this way. If you prefer, make individual puddings to serve with the roast by cooking them in a 12-hole bun tin – you'll need slightly less batter, so make it with 110g (4oz) plain flour, a pinch of salt, 1 egg and 300ml (½ pint) milk, and use about ½ teaspoon of vegetable oil in each bun tin hole.

If you follow the batter recipe here, you'll get the hang of making it by the all-in-one method, which is so quick and easy. It simply means that the batter ingredients are whisked together all at once with a balloon or spiral hand whisk. It only takes moments, and it gives you a smooth, lump-free batter, though you could whizz everything together in a blender or food processor if you prefer.

SERVES 4

Rib of beef, rolled sirloin or topside joint, *weighing at least 900g (2lb)*

Parsnips, *4 small, halved lengthways*

Carrots, *450g (1lb), sliced*

Green beans, *350g (12oz), trimmed*

Savoy or white cabbage, *a few leaves*

Cornflour, *2 tablespoons, blended with a little cold water*

Salt and freshly ground black pepper

Batter:

Plain flour, *175g (6oz)*

Salt, *¼ teaspoon*

Eggs, *2 small*

Milk, *450ml (¾ pint)*

Vegetable oil, *4 tablespoons*

1 Preheat the oven to 180°C/350°F/Gas 4. Calculate the cooking time for the meat by checking the chart below, according to the weight of the joint and how you like it to be cooked. Place the meat in a large roasting tin and put it in the oven, adding the parsnips to the roasting tin for the final 40 minutes of cooking time.

2 Next make the batter for the Yorkshire puddings. Sift the flour and salt into a large bowl, crack the eggs into the middle, then add the milk all at once. Beat to make a smooth batter using a hand whisk – this will only take a few moments. Cover the batter and leave it to stand.

3 When the meat is cooked, transfer it to a carving plate or board and cover tightly with foil, to allow it to rest in a warm place. Keep the parsnips in a warm place.

4 Increase the oven temperature to 220°C/425°F/Gas 7. Pour 1 tablespoon of oil into four 18cm (7 inch) round baking tins – sandwich tins are perfect. Put them into the oven for at least 5 minutes, so that the oil is very hot – this is important for the batter to rise successfully.

5 Remove the baking tins from the oven, pour in the batter and return them to the oven as quickly as possible, shutting the oven door swiftly. Bake the puddings for 25–30 minutes until they are well risen and golden brown.

6 Whilst the puddings are baking, cook the remaining vegetables by simmering them separately in lightly salted boiling water. The carrots will take about 15 minutes,

continued overleaf...

MEAT ROASTING TIMES:

Rare meat – 20 mins per 450g (1lb) + 20 mins

Medium – 25 mins per 450g (1lb) + 25 mins

Well done – 30 mins per 450g (1lb) + 30 mins

the beans about 6 minutes and the cabbage about 4 minutes.

7　Meanwhile, prepare the gravy. Skim off the excess fat from the roasting tin, then add 600ml (1 pint) of hot water to the roasting tin and simmer on the hob for 4–5 minutes. Stir the blended cornflour, add it to the roasting tin and stir until thickened and smooth. Season with salt and pepper, then transfer to a small saucepan and keep hot.

8　Carve the meat. Remove the Yorkshire puddings from their tins and place onto 4 warmed plates. Quickly arrange the meat and vegetables in them, and pour in some piping hot gravy.

COOK'S TIPS:

▦　Leaving the batter to stand for a while is advisable, though not essential.

▦　Avoid opening the oven door for the first 25 minutes as the puddings cook, then check quickly to see whether they are done. If they need a little longer, shut the oven door quickly – otherwise they might sink.

PEPPERED FILLET STEAK WITH MUSHROOMS AND MELTING STILTON

A fantastic recipe if you love steak and blue Stilton – the two taste terrific together.

SERVES 4

Fillet steaks,	*4, weighing 175g–225g (6–8oz) each*
Crushed black peppercorns,	*about 1 tablespoon*
Butter,	*25g (1oz)*
Vegetable oil,	*1 tablespoon*
Stilton cheese,	*75g (3oz), sliced into 4 thin wedges*
Mushrooms,	*175g (6oz), sliced*
Dijon mustard,	*2 teaspoons*
Single cream,	*150ml (5fl oz)*
Salt	

1　Cut a pocket into each fillet steak, as if you were slicing them through the middle horizontally, but without cutting them right through. Close the pockets, then sprinkle each steak with crushed peppercorns, pressing them into the surface.

2　Heat the butter in a frying pan with the vegetable oil. Add the steaks and cook to your liking – about 4 minutes for rare, 6 for medium and 8 for well done – though this will depend on the thickness of the steaks. Just before they are done, tuck a slice of Stilton into each pocket and cook for a few moments longer so that it starts to melt.

3　Lift the steaks onto warm plates and keep warm. Add the mushrooms to the frying pan, cook for 2–3 minutes then add the mustard and single cream. Heat, stirring, until just beginning to boil, then season with a little salt.

4　Spoon the mushroom cream sauce over the steaks and serve at once.

COOK'S TIP:

▦　Do make sure that the butter and oil mixture is hot before you add the steaks to the frying pan, as you want to sear them on both sides.

BEEF CASSEROLE WITH HORSERADISH AND PARSLEY DUMPLINGS

Filling and delicious, this beef stew is the definitive comfort food.

SERVES 6

Suitable for freezing

Vegetable oil, *1 tablespoon*

Bacon, *3 rashers, chopped*

Braising steak, *900g (2lb), cut into chunks*

Beef stock, *750ml (1¼ pints)*

Shallots, *12 (or 2 onions, chopped)*

Tomatoes, *2*

Garlic clove, *1, crushed*

Bay leaf, *1*

Parsnips, *2 medium, cut into chunks*

Carrots, *2, cut into chunks*

Leeks, *2, sliced*

Dumplings:

Self-raising flour, *110g (4oz)*

Parsley, *2 tablespoons, chopped*

Butter, *50g (2oz), chilled*

Creamed horseradish, *2 teaspoons*

Salt and freshly ground black pepper

1 Heat the vegetable oil in a large saucepan and add the bacon and cubes of beef a few at a time, cooking over a high heat to seal and brown them.

2 Add the beef stock and shallots or onions, whole tomatoes, garlic and bay leaf. Bring up to the boil, then reduce the heat, cover and simmer for 1¼ hours.

3 Add the parsnips, carrots and leeks. Cover and cook for a further 45 minutes, or until the meat is very tender.

4 To make the dumplings, sift the flour into a bowl and add ½ teaspoon of salt and the parsley. Coarsely grate the chilled butter and stir it through the flour, then add the horseradish and just enough cold water to make a soft dough.

5 Knead the dough lightly for a moment, then form into 12 small dumplings. Add to the casserole, letting them sit on the surface. Cover and cook for another 20 minutes, until the dumplings are light and fluffy.

6 Check the seasoning, adding salt and pepper, if needed, then remove the bay leaf.

COOK'S TIP:

▧ Serve with mashed or baked potatoes and a fresh green vegetable, such as cabbage or broccoli.

LAMB AND VEGETABLE MOUSSAKA

A fabulous aroma from this tasty dish tells you something good is cooking!

SERVES 4

Suitable for freezing

Olive oil, *2 teaspoons*

Lean minced lamb, *500g (1lb 2oz)*

Onion, *1, finely chopped*

Garlic cloves, *2, crushed*

Lamb or vegetable stock cube, *1, dissolved in 150ml (¼ pint) hot water*

Tomato purée, *2 tablespoons*

Mixed dried herbs, *1 teaspoon*

Courgette, *1, chopped*

Cornflour, *2 tablespoons, blended with a little cold water*

Aubergine, *1 small, thinly sliced*

Potato, *1 large, par-boiled and sliced*

Greek-style natural yogurt, *200g (7oz)*

Egg, *1*

Mature Cheddar cheese, *50g (2oz), grated*

Salt and freshly ground black pepper

1 Preheat the oven to 190°C/375°F/Gas 5.

2 Heat the olive oil in a large frying pan or saucepan. Add the minced lamb a handful at a time, cooking over a high heat to seal and brown it. Add the onion and garlic and cook, stirring often, for about 5 minutes.

3 Stir in the stock, tomato purée, herbs and courgette. Bring to the boil, then reduce the heat and simmer for 10 minutes without a lid. Stir in the blended cornflour and cook gently for 2 minutes, until thickened.

4 Spoon half the mince mixture into a large ovenproof baking dish. Cover with the aubergine slices. Spread the remaining mixture over them, then arrange the sliced potato on top in an overlapping layer.

5 Beat together the yogurt and egg, then stir in most of the grated cheese. Season, then spread over the potatoes. Sprinkle with the remaining cheese, then bake for about 45 minutes, until the topping is set and golden brown.

COOK'S TIP:

▪ If you're not keen on aubergine, substitute another layer of sliced par-boiled potatoes instead.

MINTY LAMB BURGERS WITH MUSTARD DRESSING

Choose lean minced lamb to make these tasty burgers, then serve with salad and a tasty mustard dressing.

SERVES 4

Suitable for freezing

Lean minced lamb, *500g (1lb 2oz)*

Spring onions, *6, trimmed and finely chopped*

Mint, *1 tablespoon, chopped*

Mixed dried herbs, *1 teaspoon*

Salt and freshly ground black pepper

Greek-style natural yogurt, *8 tablespoons*

Wholegrain mustard, *2 teaspoons*

Salad, *to serve*

Burger buns, *4*

1   In a large bowl, mix together the lamb, spring onions, mint and dried herbs. Season well with salt and pepper, then form into 4 burgers.

2   Preheat the grill. Arrange the burgers on the grill rack and cook for about 5–6 minutes on each side.

3   Meanwhile, mix together the yogurt and mustard, seasoning with a little salt and pepper.

4   Arrange the salad on the buns, top with the burgers, then finish with the mustard dressing. Serve at once.

COOK'S TIP:

▨   Freeze uncooked burgers, separating each one with a piece of freezer wrap. Freeze for up to 2 months.

LAMB CUTLETS WITH ROASTED WINTER VEGETABLES

Enjoy the heady aromas of roasting vegetables, lamb and rosemary as this wonderful dish cooks in the oven.

SERVES 4

Potatoes, *2, cut into chunks*

Carrots, *2, cut into chunks*

Parsnips, *2, cut into chunks*

Red or white onion, *1 large, cut into wedges*

Butternut squash, *350g (12oz), peeled, deseeded and cut into chunks*

Olive oil, *3 tablespoons*

Cumin seeds, *1 teaspoon (optional)*

Dried chilli flakes, *½ teaspoon (optional)*

Salt and freshly ground black pepper

Lamb cutlets, *8*

Butter, *25g (1oz), softened*

Rosemary, *2 teaspoons, chopped*

1   Preheat the oven to 200°C/400°F/Gas 6.

2   Put the potatoes, carrots, parsnips, onion and squash into a large roasting tin. Drizzle with the olive oil, add the cumin seeds and chilli flakes, if using, then season well with salt and pepper. Toss together to coat.

3   Arrange the lamb cutlets over the vegetables and season with a little more salt and pepper.

4   Mix the butter and rosemary together, then spread a little over each lamb cutlet. Transfer to the oven and roast for 45–50 minutes, turning the cutlets over halfway through the cooking time. Check that the vegetables are tender and then serve.

COOK'S TIP:

▨   Potatoes take a bit longer to roast than the other vegetables, so cut them into slightly smaller chunks. Instead of butternut squash, try sweet potatoes, celeriac or swede.

GARLIC AND ROSEMARY ROAST LAMB WITH ONION SAUCE

Leg of lamb smells and tastes fantastic when cooked with garlic and rosemary. Serve it with roast vine tomatoes and a creamy onion sauce for a wonderful meal.

SERVES 4

Leg of lamb, *1, weighing 2.25–2.5kg (5–5½lb)*

Garlic cloves, *4–5, peeled and thickly sliced*

Fresh rosemary sprigs, *a handful*

Butter, *50g (2oz)*

Small tomatoes on the vine, *about 20*

Onion, *1 large, thinly sliced*

Dark or light muscovado sugar, *1 teaspoon*

Plain flour, *25g (1oz)*

Single cream or milk, *150ml (¼ pint)*

Salt and freshly ground black pepper

1 Preheat the oven to 220°C/425°F/Gas 7.

2 Using a sharp knife, make small, deep incisions all over the lamb joint. Stuff these incisions with slices of garlic and small sprigs of rosemary. Dot half the butter over the surface of the lamb, then transfer it to a large roasting tin.

3 Roast the lamb for 25–30 minutes, then remove from the oven. Reduce the oven temperature to 170°C/325°F/Gas 3. Cover the lamb with a tent of foil, so that it barely touches the meat, then return it to the oven to cook for 2½ hours, adding the vine tomatoes to the roasting tin for the final 15–20 minutes.

4 Remove the lamb from the oven, and lift it on to a carving dish. Cover with the foil and allow the meat to rest for 10–15 minutes. Keep the tomatoes in a warm place.

5 Meanwhile, make the sauce. Skim off the excess fat from the roasting tin, then add 300ml (½ pint) of hot water to the roasting tin and simmer on the hob for 4–5 minutes.

6 Melt the remaining butter in a saucepan and cook the onion with the sugar for about 5 minutes, until golden. Add the flour and cook over a low heat for 1 minute, then gradually stir in the cream or milk. Strain in the liquid from the roasting tin, then bring up to the boil, stirring until thickened and smooth. Season.

7 Carve the lamb and serve with the roast vine tomatoes and onion sauce, accompanied by vegetables of your choice.

COOK'S TIP:

▨ Adding sugar to the onion helps it to caramelise, giving it a good flavour.

MEXICAN LAMB TORTILLAS

Try these spicy lamb meatballs with their tasty salsa – you'll love them.

SERVES 4

Suitable for freezing

Lean minced lamb, *500g (1lb 2oz)*

Onion, *1 small, finely chopped*

Ground coriander, *2 teaspoons*

Ground cumin, *1 teaspoon*

Mild chilli powder, *½ teaspoon*

Mixed dried herbs, *1 teaspoon*

Salt and freshly ground black pepper

Egg yolk, *1*

Soft tortillas, *8*

Greek-style natural yogurt, *8 tablespoons*

Salsa:

Fresh mint or coriander sprigs, *a few, chopped*

Red onion, *1 small, finely chopped*

Tomatoes, *2, finely chopped*

Cucumber, *5cm (2 inch) piece, finely chopped*

Lime or lemon juice, *1 tablespoon*

Salt and freshly ground black pepper

1 In a large bowl, mix together the minced lamb, onion, coriander, cumin, chilli powder, dried herbs, salt and pepper and egg yolk. Form into meatballs.

2 Preheat a hot grill.

3 Thread the meatballs onto kebab sticks or soaked wooden skewers and cook under the grill for about 8–10 minutes, turning occasionally.

4 Meanwhile, make the salsa by mixing together the mint or coriander, red onion, tomatoes, cucumber and lime or lemon juice. Season to taste.

5 To serve, top each tortilla with hot lamb meatballs, add a couple of tablespoons of Greek-style yogurt to each portion, and serve with the salsa.

COOK'S TIP:

 Warm the soft tortillas in a hot oven for a couple of minutes, to make them taste even better.

PORK AND APPLE SAUTÉ

Pork tenderloin – or fillet, as it is otherwise known – tastes delicious coated in herbs and cooked with onions, apple slices and cider or apple juice.

SERVES 4

Pork seasoning, *2 teaspoons*

Plain flour, *1 tablespoon*

Salt and freshly ground pink or black pepper

Pork tenderloin, *680g (1½lb), cut into 2.5cm (1 inch) slices*

Lemon juice, *1 tablespoon*

Red apple, *1, cored and sliced*

Butter, *25g (1oz)*

Olive oil, *1 tablespoon*

Onion, *1, sliced*

Garlic clove, *1, thinly sliced (optional)*

Dry cider or apple juice, *300ml (½ pint)*

Pork or chicken stock cube, *1, dissolved in 150ml (¼ pint) hot water*

Bay leaves, *2, or 2 sprigs of rosemary*

Crème fraîche or fresh soured cream, *2 tablespoons*

Fine shreds of lemon zest, *to garnish*

1　Sprinkle the pork seasoning and flour on to a plate and add a little salt and pepper. Add the pieces of pork and toss them in the seasoned flour. Put the lemon juice into a small bowl and add the apple slices, tossing them to coat.

2　Heat the butter and oil in a large frying pan or sauté pan and add the pieces of pork, frying them on both sides until well-browned. Add the onion and garlic, if using, and cook for a few more minutes.

3　Pour the cider or apple juice and stock into the pan and bring up to the boil. Add the bay leaves or rosemary and simmer for about 15–20 minutes until the liquid has reduced by half.

Drain the apple slices and add to the pan for the final few minutes.

4　Spoon the crème fraîche or soured cream into the pan and garnish with fine shreds of lemon zest. Sprinkle with a few crushed pink peppercorns or a little extra freshly ground black pepper, remove the bay leaves or rosemary sprigs, then serve.

COOK'S TIP:

▨ Pork seasoning is a tasty mixture of sage, apple, herbs and spices. Look for it in the herb and spice racks at your supermarket. If you can't find it, use a mixture of crushed dried rosemary and thyme or dried mixed herbs.

PORK, SAGE AND SMOKY BACON PARCELS

These neat and tasty pork parcels are perfect for a special meal – and they're very easy to make.

SERVES 6

Suitable for freezing

Pork fillets, *3, each weighing about 350g (12oz)*	
Fresh sage leaves, *12, + extra for garnish*	
Smoked streaky bacon, *12 rashers*	
Butter, *25g (1oz)*	
Olive oil, *1 tablespoon*	
Onions, *1 red, 1 white, sliced*	
White wine, *150ml (¼ pint)*	
Chicken stock, *150ml (¼ pint)*	
Balsamic or red wine vinegar, *2 teaspoons*	
Salt and freshly ground black pepper	

1   Rinse the pork, pat dry with kitchen paper, then cut each fillet into 4 pieces. Place a sage leaf on top of each one. Stretch out the bacon rashers using the back of a knife, then wrap one rasher around each piece of pork, tucking in the ends and securing them with cocktail sticks.

2   Heat the butter and olive oil in a large frying pan and add the pork. Seal and brown one side for a couple of minutes, then turn over and brown the other side. Add the onions and cook for about 5 minutes, stirring every now and then.

3   Pour in the wine, chicken stock and vinegar. Season with a little salt and pepper. Bring to the boil, then reduce the heat to a low simmer. Cook gently for about 20–25 minutes, without a lid, turning the pork over halfway through the cooking time. The liquid should reduce down, but do make sure that it doesn't boil dry.

4   Serve two pieces of pork per person with the onions. (Remember to remove any cocktail sticks.) Spoon over some of the reduced wine sauce, and garnish with sprigs of sage.

COOK'S TIP:

■ Try making this dish with skinless, boneless chicken breasts instead of pork – you'll need six medium ones.

GAMMON WITH CHEESE, WINE AND PRAWN SAUCE

This unusual combination may sound a little strange, yet the flavours complement each other brilliantly.

SERVES 2

Gammon steaks, *2, de-rinded*	
Milk, *200ml (⅓ pint)*	
Butter, *15g (½oz)*	
Plain flour, *15g (½oz)*	
Dry white wine, *2 tablespoons*	
Cheddar cheese, *40g (1½oz), grated*	
Peeled prawns, *75g (3oz)*	
Salt and freshly ground black pepper	

1   Preheat the grill.

2   Snip the gammon steaks at intervals around the edge where the rind has been removed to prevent them from curling too much as they cook. Place on the grill pan and grill for about 5–6 minutes on each side.

3   Meanwhile, put the milk, butter and flour into a saucepan and heat, stirring constantly with a small whisk, until the sauce thickens and boils.

4   Add the wine to the sauce and bubble up for a few moments, then reduce the heat and cook gently, stirring, for another minute. Add the cheese and prawns and cook over a gentle heat to warm through – about 2 minutes. Season to taste with salt and pepper.

5   Serve the gammon steaks, accompanied by the sauce and fresh vegetables – cauliflower and broccoli taste particularly good.

SAVOURY BREAD AND BUTTER PUDDING WITH HAM, LEEKS AND CHEESE

A terrific savoury pudding that's easy, economical and very, very tasty.

SERVES 4–6

Suitable for vegetarians, if the ham is omitted

Butter, *40g (1½oz)*

Leeks or onions, *2 medium, sliced*

Bread, *8 thin slices from a large loaf*

Cooked ham, *110g (4oz), cut into chunks*

Double Gloucester or Cheddar cheese, *150g (5oz), grated*

Milk, *600ml (1 pint)*

Eggs, *3*

Salt and freshly ground black pepper

1 Grease a 1.5 litre (2½ pint) baking dish with a little of the butter.

2 Melt the remaining butter in a frying pan and add the leeks or onions. Sauté for about 5 minutes until softened.

3 Cut the bread into triangles, then put a layer in the base of the baking dish. Scatter half the leeks or onion on top, then sprinkle with half the cooked ham and half the grated cheese. Arrange the remaining bread triangles over the surface, followed by the rest of the leeks or onions and ham.

4 Beat the milk and eggs together and season with salt and pepper. Pour evenly over the bread, then sprinkle with the remaining cheese. Cover and leave to stand for 20–30 minutes.

5 Preheat the oven to 190°C/375°F/Gas 5. Remove the cover from the pudding and bake for 30–35 minutes, until puffed-up and golden brown. Serve at once.

COOK'S TIPS:

▓ Leave the pudding to stand for just 10 minutes if you haven't got much time. Alternatively, assemble the pudding a few hours in advance, ready for baking when you need it.

▓ This is a great recipe for using up slightly stale bread – and it soaks up more moisture because of its drier texture.

▓ Try to buy just one thick slice of cooked ham rather than thin slices, then cut it into dice. You could always buy ham "off-cuts" to make the dish even more economical.

CHESHIRE POTATO CAKES WITH HAM AND PINEAPPLE

This is an excellent recipe for using up mashed potato – in a very tasty way.

SERVES 2

Butter, *25g (1oz)*

Spring onions, *4, finely chopped*

Cold mashed potato, *225g (8oz)*

Cheshire cheese, *75g (3oz) grated*

Salt and freshly ground black pepper

Egg, *1, beaten*

Plain flour, *25g (1oz)*

Roast ham, *2 slices*

Pineapple rings, *2, well drained if canned*

1   Melt the butter in a frying pan and sauté the spring onions until softened, about 3–4 minutes.
2   Mix the spring onions into the mashed potato with half the cheese. Season with salt and pepper, then form into 2 round potato cakes. Dip each one in beaten egg, then dust with flour.

3   Cook the potato cakes in the frying pan for about 10 minutes, turning once, until golden brown. Add a little more butter to the pan if necessary.
4   Meanwhile, preheat the grill.
5   Top each potato cake with a slice of ham, folding it to fit. Pop a pineapple ring on top, then sprinkle with the remaining cheese. Grill until golden brown and bubbling, then serve at once.

COOK'S TIPS:

▓ Fresh pineapple gives the best flavour, though canned pineapple rings in natural juice are more convenient. Choose whichever you prefer.

▓ Lancashire, Wensleydale or white Stilton could all be used instead of Cheshire cheese.

BACON CHOPS WITH SULTANA AND ORANGE SAUCE

Caramelised shallots make the basis for a delicious sauce to serve with bacon chops or gammon.

SERVES 4

Butter, *25g (1oz)*

Shallots, *12, peeled and halved*

Light or dark muscovado sugar, *1 teaspoon*

Orange zest, *1 tablespoon, finely shredded*

Orange juice, *200ml (⅓ pint)*

Sultanas or raisins, *25g (1oz)*

Cinnamon stick, *1 (or use a pinch of ground cinnamon)*

Ground mixed spice, *a good pinch*

Bacon chops or gammon steaks, *4*

Cornflour, *2 teaspoons, blended with a little cold water*

Salt and freshly ground black pepper

1   Melt the butter in a heavy-based saucepan and add the shallots. Cook them over a low heat for about 10–15 minutes until they turn a rich, golden brown.
2   Add the sugar, orange zest, orange juice and sultanas or raisins to the saucepan with the cinnamon and mixed spice. Heat and simmer very gently for about 12 minutes whilst you cook the bacon chops or gammon.
3   Preheat the grill. Snip the bacon chops or gammon steaks at intervals around the edge where the rind has been removed. This prevents them from curling up too much as they cook. Place on the grill pan and grill for about 5–6 minutes on each side.
4   Add the blended cornflour to the sauce and cook gently until thickened. Simmer for a few moments, season to taste, then serve with the bacon chops or gammon.

COOK'S TIP:

▓ A splash of Cointreau or Grand Marnier added to the sauce makes it taste extra special – add it with the sugar and orange juice.

SAUSAGE AND ONION SUPPER WITH GARLIC MASH

With a little tweaking, even the most ordinary foods can taste fantastic. Here's proof!

SERVES 4

Butter, *50g (2oz)*

Onion, *1 large, sliced*

Sausages, *8*

Red wine, *150ml (¼ pint)*

Vegetable or chicken stock cube, *1, dissolved in 300ml (½ pint) hot water*

Italian mixed dried herbs, *1 teaspoon*

Dried porcini mushrooms, *1 x 10g pack*

Potatoes, *900g (2lb)*

Garlic cloves, *2, crushed*

Milk, *4–5 tablespoons*

Parsley, *3 tablespoons, chopped*

Salt and freshly ground black pepper

1 Melt half the butter in a large frying pan and add the onion. Cook over a low heat for about 10 minutes until golden brown. Push to one side of the pan and add the sausages, cooking and turning them until browned – about 5 minutes.

2 Add the wine to the frying pan and let it bubble up for a minute or two. Pour in the hot stock and add the dried herbs and mushrooms. Bring up to the boil, then reduce the heat and simmer gently for 20 minutes, to reduce the liquid by about one third.

3 Meanwhile, cook the potatoes in plenty of lightly salted boiling water until tender.

4 Melt the remaining butter and fry the garlic for 2–3 minutes. Drain and mash the potatoes, then beat in the garlic, butter, milk and parsley. Season, reheat for a few moments, then serve with the sausages.

COOK'S TIP:

■ Use 110g (4oz) sliced fresh mushrooms instead of the dried ones. If you wish, omit the wine, add a little extra stock and flavour it with 3–4 tablespoons of medium sherry.

fish and shellfish

If ever you've been short of ideas when it comes to cooking fish, look no further. Be inspired by the wonderful recipes here – all designed to put some great tastes on your plate. And look at the colours too! If you thought that fish was unexciting, now's the time for a serious rethink.

Fish is perfect for today's busy lifestyles. It cooks quickly and tastes delicious – especially when you complement it with other interesting flavours. Take the recipe for Roast Mediterranean Fish on Rustic Bread, for instance – it's ideal for a special occasion, and the flavour is superb. There are some classic fish dishes in this chapter too. Our opening recipe holds your hand as you get the hang of making a seriously good fish pie – then later there's the low-down on making a perfect hollandaise sauce to serve with salmon or trout. Everything you'll ever need!

Getting the hang of...

FISH PIE

Fish pie is a classic British recipe, and it is truly wonderful. Homely and comforting, it makes the most of nutritious fish in a very tasty way. You can use your own choice of fish to make this pie, according to its availability, the occasion and your budget. If it's for a family supper, you could just use coley, pollack or whiting and smoked haddock – and forget the prawns altogether. If you're making the pie for a real feast, push the boat out and use the varieties suggested.

Home-made fish pie is fantastic, so if you've never made one before, follow these instructions to discover a new favourite. And if you haven't made one for ages, you must try this recipe to remind yourself just how delicious a fish pie can be.

SERVES 4

Suitable for freezing

Potatoes, *900g (2lb)*	
Fresh fish fillets (cod, smoked haddock, salmon), *900g (2lb) in total*	
Milk, *450ml (¾ pint)*	
Butter, *75g (3oz)*	
Salt and freshly ground black pepper	
Parsley sprigs, *a few*	
Large peeled prawns, *175g (6oz), defrosted if frozen*	
Onion, *1 small, chopped*	
Leek, *1, trimmed and sliced*	
Plain flour, *40g (1½oz)*	

1 Put the potatoes on to boil with a good pinch of salt. Simmer them until tender.

2 Put the fish into a large frying pan with deep sides – or use a wok. Add the milk and 15g (½oz) of the butter. Season and add the parsley sprigs. Bring to simmering point, then cover and poach gently for 6–8 minutes, until the fish is just cooked. The flesh should be opaque and the flakes should separate when tested with a fork.

3 Lift the fish from the pan on to a plate, draining it well and reserving the cooking liquid. Cool for a few minutes, then break it up into chunks. Transfer it to a buttered 2 litre (3½ pint) baking dish, making sure that the different types of fish are evenly mixed. Scatter the prawns over the top.

4 Cook the onion and leek in lightly salted boiling water for about 5 minutes, until just tender. Drain, reserving the cooking liquid. Mix the leeks and onion with the fish.

5 Preheat the oven to 190°C/375°F/Gas 5.

6 Measure the stock from the cooked fish and make it up to 450ml (¾ pint) with liquid from cooking the vegetables. Don't worry if there are any bits of fish floating around in it, they will be mixed into the sauce.

7 Melt 40g (1½oz) of the butter in a saucepan. Stir in the flour and cook gently over a low heat for about 1 minute, until it looks grainy. Remove from the heat and gradually add the liquid. Return to the heat and cook gently, stirring, until thickened. Pour into the dish, allowing it to seep into the fish mixture. Avoid adding too much, or else it could overflow during baking.

8 Mash the potatoes, adding a splash of milk, a knob of butter and some salt and pepper. Pile or pipe on top of the fish and dot with any remaining butter. Bake for about 45 minutes, until piping hot and browned on the surface.

COOK'S TIPS:

▓ Cod, smoked haddock and salmon make an excellent combination of fish – though you can choose any variety you like.

▓ Select a floury variety of potato, suitable for mashing. Check the packaging or ask your greengrocer when choosing them.

POTTED SMOKED FISH WITH PRAWNS

In this recipe, smoked haddock from the fresh fish counter is poached and cooled, then combined with smoked mackerel, which you buy from the delicatessen section and doesn't need cooking.

SERVES 6

Smoked haddock, *225g (8oz)*

Smoked mackerel, *225g (8oz)*

Greek-style natural yogurt, *4 tablespoons*

Lemon juice, *2 teaspoons*

Parsley, *2 tablespoons, finely chopped*

Peeled prawns, *150g (5oz), defrosted if frozen*

Butter, *50g (2oz)*

Bay leaves or lemon wedges, *to garnish*

Brown bread and butter, *to serve*

1   Poach the smoked haddock in a shallow pan with just enough water to cover it. It should take about 6 minutes. To check that it is cooked, test it with a fork – it should flake easily. Drain well, allow it to cool, then flake the fish, removing any skin and bones.

2   Remove the skin and any bones from the smoked mackerel. Put the fish into a mixing bowl and flake with a fork. Add the haddock, yogurt, lemon juice and most of the parsley.

3   Divide the mixture between 6 individual serving pots or ramekins. Top with the prawns, piling them into the middle.

4   Melt the butter, then drizzle over the prawns. Add a bay leaf or lemon wedge to each pot and scatter with the remaining parsley. Chill until ready to serve, then use to spread generously on to brown bread and butter.

COOK'S TIP:

▓ The haddock and mackerel make a delicious combination, though you could use just one variety if you prefer, using 450g (1lb) of fish in total.

SMOKED HADDOCK WITH HERB BUTTER AND BACON BITS

Some of the best fish recipes are the simplest – this one is a perfect case in point.

SERVES 4

Butter, *50g (2oz), softened*

Fresh mixed herbs, *2 tablespoons, finely chopped*

Streaky bacon, *4 rashers*

Smoked haddock fillets, *4, each weighing about 175g–225g (6–8oz)*

Lemon or lime juice, *2 tablespoons*

Salt and freshly ground black pepper

Savoy or white cabbage, *½ medium, shredded*

Leeks, *2, finely sliced*

Fresh herb sprigs, *to garnish*

1 Reserve 15g (½oz) of butter. Put the remainder into a mixing bowl, add the chopped fresh herbs and beat them into the butter.

2 Preheat the grill. Cook the bacon until crispy, then drain on kitchen paper and set aside.

3 Arrange the fish fillets on the grill rack and spread them with the herb butter. Sprinkle with the lemon or lime juice and season with black pepper.

4 Grill for 6–8 minutes, until the fish is cooked. Test with a fork to check – the flesh should be opaque and flake easily.

5 Meanwhile, lightly cook the cabbage and leeks in a little boiling, salted water. Drain well and add the reserved butter. Pile onto warmed plates and top with the grilled fish. Crumble the bacon rashers on top and garnish with fresh herb sprigs.

COOK'S TIP:

■ There's no need to add salt to the fish – it's already quite salty, so just season with black pepper.

SALMON STEAKS WITH LIME HONEY BUTTER

Fresh salmon is more affordable these days, so why not try it marinated in a wonderful mixture of white wine, honey, lime juice and dill?

SERVES 4

Salmon steaks, *4, weighing 150–175g (5–6oz) each*

Dry white wine, *200ml (⅓ pint)*

Clear honey, *2 tablespoons*

Lime, *1, finely grated zest and juice*

Salt, *good pinch*

Peppercorns, *1 teaspoon*

Fresh dill or parsley, *1 tablespoon, chopped*

Butter, *25g (1oz)*

1 Rinse the salmon steaks and put them into a shallow, non-metallic dish. Mix together the wine, honey, lime zest and juice, salt, peppercorns and herbs, stirring for a few moments to dissolve the honey. Pour over the fish, then cover and leave to marinate for at least 1 hour.

2 Preheat the grill. Arrange the salmon steaks on the grill pan and brush with melted butter.

Cook for about 3–4 minutes, depending on their thickness. Turn the salmon over, then brush with butter once more. Grill for 5 minutes or so until the fish is cooked.

3 To check that the fish is done, test with a fork to see that the flakes separate easily, and make sure that the flesh is opaque.

4 Whilst the fish is cooking, heat the marinade with any remaining butter until bubbling, then turn the heat to low.

5 Transfer the salmon steaks to warmed plates and drizzle the hot marinade over them. Serve with vegetables and buttered new potatoes.

COOK'S TIP:

▪ A zester is a very useful little gadget, ideal for removing the zest from citrus fruits without getting any of the white pith, which adds bitterness.

FRESH TROUT WITH WATERCRESS SAUCE

Fresh trout is widely available and so easy to cook – serve with a simple sauce flavoured with watercress and orange zest.

SERVES 4

Butter, *15g (½oz), melted*	
Olive oil, *1 tablespoon*	
Fresh trout fillets, *4, weighing about 175g (6oz) each*	
Orange, *1, finely grated zest and juice*	
Parsley, *1 tablespoon, finely chopped*	
Salt and freshly ground black pepper	
Low-fat soft cheese with garlic and herbs, *200g (7oz)*	
Low-fat plain fromage frais, *110g (4oz)*	
Watercress, *50g (2oz) finely chopped*	

1   Heat the butter and olive oil in a large frying pan and add the trout fillets, skin side uppermost. Cook them for about 6–8 minutes, turning once and basting from time to time with the pan juices.

2   Add the orange juice and parsley to the frying pan and bubble up for a few moments. Season with salt and pepper, then turn the heat to low whilst you make the sauce.

3   Put the soft cheese, fromage frais, orange zest and watercress into a saucepan. Heat gently, stirring occasionally, until melted and smooth. Season with salt and pepper.

4   Serve the trout fillets, accompanied by the sauce.

COOK'S TIP:

▓ Serve the trout fillets on a bed of lightly cooked asparagus spears, courgettes or green beans.

PRAWN AND PAPAYA SALAD WITH LIME YOGURT DRESSING

Papaya – or paw paw as it is otherwise called – tastes delicious in this refreshing salad.

SERVES 4

Carrot, *1, peeled*

Cucumber, *10cm (4 inch) piece*

Sesame oil, *1 tablespoon*

Natural low-fat yogurt, *5 tablespoons*

Lime, *1, finely grated zest and juice*

Salt and freshly ground black pepper

Romaine or cos lettuce, *1, shredded*

Papaya, *1, peeled, deseeded and sliced*

Large peeled prawns, *350g (12oz), defrosted if frozen*

Basil leaves, *to garnish*

1   Pare the carrot and cucumber into long strips, using a potato peeler. Put them into a very large bowl of cold water and chill in the refrigerator for about 30 minutes to make them crisp and curly.

2   To make the dressing, whisk together the sesame oil, yogurt, lime zest, lime juice and seasoning.

3   Divide the lettuce between 4 serving plates and arrange the papaya on top. Drain the carrot and cucumber thoroughly and divide between the salads. Top with the prawns, spoon over the dressing and garnish with basil leaves.

PLAICE WITH ORANGE, THYME AND BASIL STUFFING

Roll up some plaice fillets with a tasty herb and orange filling for an easy dish that's suitable for a starter or main course.

SERVES 4

Suitable for freezing

Plaice fillets, *4 large*

Butter, *50g (2oz)*

Onion, *1 small, finely chopped*

Fresh white breadcrumbs, *110g (4oz)*

Oranges, *2, finely grated zest and juice*

Basil leaves, *a few, torn into pieces*

Thyme leaves, *2 teaspoons (or 1 teaspoon of dried thyme)*

Egg yolk, *1*

Salt and freshly ground black pepper

Dry white wine, vermouth or Grand Marnier, *3 tablespoons (optional)*

Thyme sprigs or basil leaves, *to garnish*

1   Preheat the oven to 180°C/350°F/Gas 4.

2   Rinse the plaice fillets and lay them on to a work surface, skin side up.

3   Melt half the butter in a small frying pan and sauté the onion gently for about 5 minutes, until softened. Add to the breadcrumbs with the orange zest, basil, thyme and egg yolk. Season with salt and pepper, then mix thoroughly to bind together.

4   Divide the stuffing between the fish, placing the mixture at the wide end of the fillets, then roll them up. Place them in a buttered baking dish, tucking the ends underneath.

5   Melt the remaining butter and add the orange juice and wine, vermouth or Grand Marnier, if using. Pour over the fish fillets and bake for 15–20 minutes, until the flesh is opaque.

6   Serve, garnished with thyme sprigs or basil leaves.

COOK'S TIP:

■   For convenience, use dried herbs – just add 2 teaspoons of mixed dried Italian herbs to the breadcrumb mixture instead of the basil and thyme.

ROAST MEDITERRANEAN FISH ON RUSTIC BREAD

Easy, yet deliciously different – that's the essence of this tasty fish dish.

SERVES 4

Butter, *50g (2oz)*

Olive oil, *2 tablespoons*

Garlic cloves, *2, finely sliced*

Aubergine, *1 small, finely chopped*

Spring onions, *1 bunch, trimmed and finely chopped*

Tomatoes, *2 large, skinned and chopped*

Sun-dried tomato paste, *2 tablespoons*

Lemon juice or vinegar, *a few drops*

Salt and freshly ground black pepper

Rustic-style bread, *4 thick slices*

Cod, haddock or sea bass, *4 x 200g (7oz) fillets*

Basil sprigs, *to garnish*

1 Preheat the oven to 190°C/375°F/Gas 5.
2 Heat the butter and olive oil in a frying pan and add the garlic, aubergine and spring onions, sautéing them over a medium-low heat until very soft, about 5–6 minutes.
3 Stir the chopped tomatoes and sun-dried tomato paste into the aubergine mixture. Add the lemon juice or vinegar and season to taste.
4 Spread the pieces of bread with half the aubergine mixture, then place in a baking dish or roasting pan. Top each one with a piece of fish, then spread the remaining aubergine mixture on top. Bake for 18–20 minutes, or until the fish is cooked. Serve, garnished with basil sprigs.

SALMON STEAKS WITH HOLLANDAISE SAUCE

Hollandaise sauce is the perfect accompaniment to poached, steamed or microwaved salmon. Here's the recipe for perfect results.

SERVES 4

Salmon fillets, *4 medium*

White wine vinegar, *3 tablespoons*

Bay leaf, *1*

Black peppercorns, *6*

Egg yolks, *3*

Unsalted butter, *150g (5oz), cut into small pieces*

Salt

1 Poach or steam the salmon steaks for about 12 minutes, or until the flesh looks opaque and flakes easily when tested with a fork. Alternatively, you could cook the fish in a microwave oven for about 4 minutes on HIGH, though check your owner's handbook for best results.
2 Meanwhile, make the hollandaise sauce. Boil the vinegar with 1 tablespoon of water, the bay leaf and peppercorns until the liquid has reduced down to about 1 tablespoon. Cool.
3 Whisk the egg yolks in a large heatproof basin and strain in the vinegar. Set the bowl over a pan of simmering water and whisk in pieces of the butter, a little at a time, until all the butter is incorporated and the sauce is the consistency of mayonnaise. Add a little salt, then keep warm, stirring often.
4 Serve the salmon steaks with the warm hollandaise, with fresh green vegetables and new potatoes.

COOK'S TIP:

▨ You must concentrate when making the sauce – any distractions, and it could curdle. Take care that you don't overheat it.

SKATE WITH WHITE WINE AND SEAFOOD SAUCE

Skate "wings" are quick and easy to cook – all you need do is brush them with butter and grill them, though they taste even better with this delicious sauce.

SERVES 4

Butter, *50g (2oz)*

Skate wings, *4*

Salt and freshly ground black pepper

Dry white wine, *150ml (¼ pint)*

Parsley, *1 tablespoon, chopped*

Mussels in shells, *350g (12oz)*

Plain flour, *25g (1oz)*

Milk, *200ml (⅓ pint)*

Peeled prawns, *50g (2oz), defrosted if frozen*

Squid rings, *110g (4oz)*

Parsley sprigs, *to garnish*

1 Preheat the grill and cover the grill rack with foil.

2 Melt 25g (1oz) of the butter. Arrange the skate wings on the grill rack and brush with the melted butter. Season with a little salt and pepper, then grill for about 8–10 minutes, turning once, until the fish is opaque.

3 Meanwhile, heat the wine in a saucepan with the chopped parsley and any remaining melted butter. Add the mussels, discarding any that remain open when tapped, then cover and cook for 3–4 minutes. Discard any mussels that fail to open.

4 Whilst the mussels are cooking, put the remaining butter into a saucepan with the flour and milk. Heat, stirring constantly with a small wire whisk, until the sauce is smooth and thick. Add the prawns and squid rings and cook gently for 2 minutes.

5 Strain the cooking liquid from the mussels into the sauce. Stir and heat for a few moments, then season and serve with the skate and mussels, garnished with parsley sprigs.

COOK'S TIP:

▇ Use 225g (8oz) of seafood cocktail rather than buying the mussels, prawns and squid separately. Simmer it with the wine and chopped parsley for about 2 minutes, then add to the white sauce.

3   In a large serving bowl, mix together the sesame or olive oil with the lime juice, chives and half the coriander. Add the drained, hot potatoes and allow to cool for 5–10 minutes.
4   Make the dressing in a small bowl by mixing together the crème fraîche or soured cream with the lime zest and remaining coriander. Season with a little salt and pepper.
5   To complete the salad, add the asparagus or green beans, red onion, red pepper and prawns to the potatoes. Season with salt and pepper and toss together. Serve with the lime and coriander dressing.

COOK'S TIP:

▓ If you're not keen on coriander, use basil or flat leaf parsley instead.

PRAWN, RED ONION AND BABY NEW POTATO SALAD

This salad bursts with fabulous colours and delicious flavours – you must try it!

SERVES 4

Baby new potatoes, *500g (1lb 2oz)*

Asparagus or fine green beans, *110g (4oz), sliced into short lengths*

Sesame oil or olive oil, *1 tablespoon*

Lime, *1, finely grated zest and juice*

Chives, *1 tablespoon, chopped*

Coriander, *2 tablespoons, chopped*

Crème fraîche or soured cream, *150g (5oz)*

Salt and freshly ground black pepper

Red onion, *1 small, thinly sliced*

Red pepper, *1 small, deseeded and thinly sliced*

Peeled prawns, *225g (8oz), defrosted if frozen*

1   Cook the potatoes in lightly salted boiling water for 15–20 minutes, until tender.
2   Meanwhile, lightly cook the asparagus or fine green beans in a small amount of water for about 4 minutes, until just cooked. Drain and rinse with cold water to cool quickly.

CHAR-GRILLED TUNA STEAKS WITH BUTTERED VEGETABLES

Tuna or swordfish steaks are readily available these days. They have a deliciously meaty texture – so try them in this Thai-style recipe.

SERVES 4

Tuna or swordfish steaks, *4, defrosted if frozen*

Vegetable oil, *2 tablespoons*

Thai fish sauce or light soy sauce, *1 tablespoon*

Lime or lemon juice, *1 tablespoon*

Salt and freshly ground black pepper

Butter, *25g (1oz)*

Garlic clove, *1, thinly sliced*

Shallots, *2, thinly sliced*

Yellow or red pepper, *1, deseeded and sliced*

Red chilli, *1 large, deseeded and sliced*

Pak choi or Chinese leaves, *175g (6oz)*

Thai 7-spice or Chinese 5-spice seasoning, *1 teaspoon*

Coriander sprigs, *to garnish*

1   Preheat a char-grill pan – this is a heavy based frying pan with ridges in it, for cooking steaks, chops and meaty-textured fish. Alternatively, use a regular heavy-based frying pan. Brush the fish steaks liberally with the oil.

2 Cook the tuna or swordfish steaks for about
3–4 minutes per side, depending on their
thickness. Sprinkle with Thai fish sauce or soy
sauce and lime or lemon juice. Season with salt
and pepper.

3 Heat the butter and any remaining oil together
in a wok or large frying pan. Add the garlic and
all the vegetables and sauté for 4–5 minutes. Add
the 7-spice or 5-spice seasoning and stir through
the vegetables with a little salt and pepper.

4 Divide the vegetables between four warmed
plates and serve with the fish steaks. Garnish
with sprigs of coriander.

COOK'S TIP:

■ Fish sauce is a dark, salty sauce with a thin
consistency, used extensively in Thai cuisine. Look for it in
oriental food shops, delicatessen and supermarkets. If you
can't find it, use soy sauce instead.

ROAST COD WITH BUTTERED PRAWN, PARSLEY AND CHEDDAR TOPPING

An easy fish dish that is baked in the oven for a few minutes, then finished off under the grill.

SERVES 6

Olive oil, *1 tablespoon*

Cod fillets, *6, weighing 175g–225g (6–8oz) each*

Butter, *50g (2oz)*

Onion, *1 small, finely chopped*

Egg, *1*

Fresh white breadcrumbs, *75g (3oz)*

Prawns, *175g (6oz)*

Mature Cheddar cheese, *50g (2oz), grated*

Parsley, *2 tablespoons, finely chopped*

Salt and freshly ground black pepper

1   Preheat the oven to 200°C/400°F/Gas 6.

2   Grease a large roasting pan or baking dish with the olive oil. Rinse the cod fillets, pat dry with kitchen paper and arrange in the roasting pan or dish.

3   Melt the butter and sauté the onion gently until softened, but not browned. Allow to cool slightly.

4   Beat the egg in a mixing bowl. Add the breadcrumbs, onion and butter, prawns, cheese and parsley. Season with salt and pepper. Mix together, then divide equally between the fish fillets, piling the mixture on top. Cover the fish loosely with a large piece of foil, then bake in the oven for 10 minutes. Meanwhile, preheat the grill.

5   Transfer the roasting pan to the grill and cook the fish for a further 2–3 minutes, until the topping browns lightly. Serve at once, with fresh vegetables.

COOK'S TIP:

▪ Instead of Cheddar, use a tasty Lancashire or Cheshire cheese – both work equally well.

SEA BASS WITH TOMATOES, COURGETTES AND PEPPERS

Fish tastes fantastic with these colourful vegetables, sautéed in butter and stir-fry oil, which is flavoured with garlic and spices.

SERVES 4

Butter, *50g (2oz)*

Stir-fry oil, *2 tablespoons*

Sea bass or cod, *4 x 200g (7oz) fillets*

Courgette, *1 large, chopped*

Red pepper, *1, deseeded and sliced*

Yellow pepper, *1, deseeded and sliced*

Tomatoes, *8 small, halved*

Lemon juice, *1 tablespoon*

Salt and freshly ground black pepper

Parsley sprigs, *to garnish*

1   Heat half the butter and oil in a very large frying pan and add the fish fillets. Cook for about 6–8 minutes, turning once, until the flesh is opaque and flakes easily when tested with a fork.

2   Lift the fish fillets from the frying pan and keep them in a warm place. Wipe out the pan with kitchen paper, then add the remaining butter and oil.

3   Sauté the courgette and peppers briskly for 3–4 minutes, then add the tomatoes and cook for another 2 minutes. Season with lemon juice, salt and pepper.

4   Divide the vegetables between 4 warmed plates. Top with the fish fillets and serve, garnished with parsley sprigs.

COOK'S TIP:

▨ Stir-fry oil is infused with the flavour of garlic, ginger and spices. Look out for it in the oriental foods section of your supermarket, or alongside other oils. If you can't find it, use sesame or olive oil instead, and sauté the vegetables with a crushed garlic clove and a pinch of ground ginger.

SALMON NIÇOISE WITH LEMON BUTTER DRESSING

Make this delicious salad with crispy lettuce and watercress, lightly cooked green beans and hard-boiled egg – with canned salmon for convenience.

SERVES 4

Fine green beans, *175g (6oz)*

Butter, *25g (1oz), melted*

Lemon, *1, finely grated zest + 1 tablespoon of juice*

Wholegrain mustard, *1 teaspoon*

Salt and freshly ground black pepper

New potatoes, *450g (1lb), halved and cooked*

Rocket or watercress, *50g (2oz)*

Cos or Romaine lettuce, *1, roughly shredded*

Tomatoes, *4, cut into wedges*

Pitted black olives, *about 20*

Eggs, *4, hard-boiled and quartered*

Red salmon, *1 x 418g can, drained*

Fresh parsley, *chopped, to garnish*

1 Cook the beans in lightly salted boiling water until just tender – about 4–5 minutes.

2 Whilst the beans are cooking, make up the dressing by whisking together the warm butter, lemon zest and juice, mustard and seasoning in a small saucepan. Keep warm.

3 Drain the beans and add to the potatoes with the dressing, tossing to coat. Allow to cool for a few minutes.

4 Meanwhile, arrange the rocket or watercress, lettuce and tomatoes on four serving plates. Divide the warm beans between them, then top each salad with the olives and quartered eggs.

5 Remove any skin from the salmon and break it up into chunks. Divide between the salads and serve, sprinkled with chopped parsley.

COOK'S TIP:

▧ Don't throw out the softened bones from canned salmon – eat them! They're an excellent source of calcium.

pasta

It's hard to believe just how quickly we have adopted pasta as one of our most popular foods. And how good it tastes with delicious dairy products! You only have to think of a classic Lasagne or Spaghetti Carbonara to realise that pasta and dairy foods make a very happy marriage. And just in case you want confirmation, both those recipes are contained within these pages.

Pasta is incredibly versatile – use it in soups, starters, salads and main courses. Do try the tasty recipe for Minestrone on page 96 – it has already become a favourite. And for a speedy evening meal, there's Salami, Lemon and Asparagus Pasta or Quick Prawn and Crab Supper. If you're a vegetarian, don't miss the recipe for Summer Vegetable Pasta – it's a real winner, and meat-eaters will love it too.

Getting the hang of...

It's amazing how so many pasta dishes have become a regular part of our meal times, and there's no doubt that lasagne always makes a welcome appearance. If you've never made it before, then you'll find this recipe straightforward and easy to follow, giving you a guaranteed result every time.

As with any recipe, choose your ingredients with care. For instance, quality lean minced beef will give a good flavour, and mature Cheddar adds extra edge to the sauce, so use these if you want the best flavour. If you don't eat meat and you want to make a vegetarian version, you could substitute Quorn mince for the beef – the lasagne will still be really tasty. And if you don't eat red meat, try turkey mince instead. Incidentally, lasagne freezes well, so why not double up the quantities and make an extra one for eating at a later date?

LASAGNE

Lasagne is a real family favourite – most children seem to love it, and it's filling and tasty. So get the hang of it with our delicious recipe.

SERVES 4–6

Suitable for freezing

Olive oil, *1 tablespoon*

Lean minced beef, *450g (1lb)*

Onion, *1, chopped*

Garlic cloves, *2, crushed*

Chopped tomatoes, *2 x 400g cans*

Italian mixed dried herbs, *1 tablespoon*

Salt and freshly ground black pepper

Lasagne sheets, *6–8, (choose ones that do not need pre-cooking)*

Cheese sauce:

Milk, *450ml (¾ pint)*

Plain flour, *40g (1½oz)*

Butter, *25g (1oz)*

Mature Cheddar cheese, *150g (5oz), grated*

1 Heat the olive oil in a large saucepan, then over a high heat add the mince a handful at a time. This is important as it seals and browns the meat to give it a good flavour.
2 Add the onion and garlic to the saucepan and cook gently for 3–4 minutes, then add the chopped tomatoes. Bring up to the boil, then reduce the heat. Add the dried herbs, then simmer for 15–20 minutes without a lid, so that the liquid reduces. Season to taste.

3 Preheat the oven to 180°C/350°F/Gas 4.
4 To make the cheese sauce, put the milk, flour and butter into a saucepan and heat, whisking constantly with a wire whisk until the sauce boils and thickens. Turn down the heat to low and cook gently for another minute. Remove from the heat and add half the grated cheese. Stir thoroughly so that the heat of the sauce melts the cheese – there's no need to return it to the hob. Season to taste with salt and pepper.
5 Pour half the mince mixture into a large rectangular baking dish. Cover with half the lasagne sheets. Spoon over half the cheese sauce and spread over the lasagne. Repeat the layers, finishing with the cheese sauce. Sprinkle the remaining cheese evenly over the top.
6 Bake for 45–50 minutes, until golden brown. Serve with salad and crusty bread.

COOK'S TIPS:

▪ For a vegetarian lasagne use frozen or reconstituted dried vegetarian mince or Quorn to make the recipe.

▪ To freeze lasagne, cool quickly, then freeze as soon as you can. Wrap in freezer wrap – or transfer to a polythene box – and freeze for up to 2 months.

SMOKY BACON, MUSHROOM AND BRIE PASTA

Try this delicious pasta dish, fired with the flavour of a little fresh chilli.

SERVES 4

Suitable for freezing

Vegetable oil, *1 tablespoon*

Fresh red chillies, *2, halved lengthways*

Pasta shapes, *175g (6oz)*

Smoked bacon rashers, *175g (6oz), de-rinded and chopped*

Onion, *1, chopped*

Garlic clove, *1, crushed*

Red pepper, *1, deseeded and sliced*

Baby plum or cherry tomatoes, *12, halved*

Mushrooms, *110g (4oz)*

Italian mixed dried herbs, *2 teaspoons*

Salt and freshly ground black pepper

Green or red pesto sauce, *3 tablespoons*

Somerset brie, *175g (6oz), cut into chunks*

Fresh herbs, *to garnish*

1 Heat the oil in a large frying pan and add the halved chillies. Sizzle them for a few moments until they begin to brown, then remove from the pan and drain on kitchen paper.

2 Put the pasta on to cook in plenty of lightly salted boiling water for about 8–10 minutes, until just tender (or cook according to pack instructions).

3 Meanwhile, add the bacon, onion and garlic to the frying pan and cook until lightly browned. Add the red pepper and cook gently for another few minutes.

4 Add the tomatoes, mushrooms, dried herbs and seasoning to the frying pan. Cook, stirring often, for 2–3 minutes.

5 Drain the pasta well, then return it to the saucepan. Add the bacon and vegetable mixture, the pesto sauce and the chunks of brie. Heat and stir so that the cheese starts to melt.

6 Share the pasta between 4 warmed serving plates. Serve at once, garnished with the chillies and fresh herbs.

COOK'S TIP:

■ Leave out the chillies if you prefer, or pep up the pasta with a few drops of hot chilli sauce.

MACARONI CHEESE WITH TOMATOES

Add a little extra to a basic macaroni cheese with a layer of chopped ham, and a topping of croûtons and sliced tomatoes.

SERVES 4

Suitable for vegetarians (see cook's tip)
Suitable for freezing

Macaroni, *350g (12oz)*	
Butter, *50g (2oz)*	
Onion, *1 small, finely chopped*	
Plain flour, *75g (3oz)*	
Milk, *900ml (1½ pints)*	
Extra Mature Cheddar cheese, *300g (11oz), grated*	
Salt and freshly ground black pepper	
English mustard, *1–2 teaspoons*	
Cooked ham, *175g (6oz), chopped (optional)*	
Croûtons, *3 tablespoons*	
Tomatoes, *2, sliced*	
Basil sprigs, *to garnish*	

1   Bring a large saucepan of water up to the boil and add half a teaspoon of salt. Tip in the macaroni, give it a good stir and bring back to the boil. Cook without a lid for 8–10 minutes, or according to pack instructions, until tender.
2   Meanwhile, melt the butter in a large saucepan and sauté the onion for 3–4 minutes, until softened, but not brown. Remove from the heat and stir in the flour. Return to the heat and cook gently for about 1 minute, stirring, until the mixture has a sandy texture.
3   Remove from the heat and gradually add the milk, stirring it in to blend. Heat, stirring constantly, until thickened and smooth, then cook gently for another minute. Remove from the heat and add about two thirds of the cheese. Season with salt, pepper and mustard.
4   Preheat a medium hot grill and warm a heatproof serving dish with a capacity of about 1.75 litres (3 pints), or use individual serving dishes.
5   Drain the cooked pasta thoroughly and stir it into the hot cheese sauce. Check the seasoning, then tip half the mixture into the warmed baking dish. Sprinkle the ham over the top, if using, then pour over the remaining macaroni cheese.
6   Scatter the croûtons and reserved cheese over the surface and top with the sliced tomatoes. Grill for about 5–8 minutes until the cheese is bubbling and golden brown. Serve, garnished with basil sprigs.

COOK'S TIPS:

■   Use a tubular pasta such as penne or rigatoni instead of macaroni. Take care not to overcook it – it needs to retain a little "bite".

■   If you are vegetarian, omit the cooked ham and substitute a layer of leeks, courgettes, peppers or mushrooms, lightly sautéed in butter to soften them.

BRIE, TUNA AND AVOCADO SALAD

Enjoy the fabulous flavour combinations in this easy, Italian-style salad.

SERVES 4–6

Pasta bows (farfalle), *150g (5oz)*	
Lemon juice, *3 tablespoons*	
Olive oil, *2 tablespoons*	
Salt and freshly ground black pepper	
Tomatoes, *2 large, sliced into wedges*	
Cucumber, *½, chopped*	
Red onion, *½, thinly sliced*	
Avocado, *1 large, peeled, stoned and sliced*	
Tuna in olive oil or brine, *1 x 400g can, drained*	
Somerset brie, *110g (4oz), cut into small chunks*	
Olives, *about a dozen (optional)*	

1   Cook the pasta bows in plenty of lightly salted boiling water for about 8–10 minutes, or according to pack instructions, until tender.

2   Meanwhile, in a large bowl, mix together the lemon juice and olive oil. Season with salt and pepper.

3   Add the tomatoes, cucumber, red onion and avocado. Break up the tuna into large chunks and add to the bowl with the brie and olives, if using.

4   Rinse the cooked pasta in cold water to cool quickly, then drain really well and add to the salad. Toss everything together gently, then serve.

COOK'S TIP:

▨   Olives are often sold in jars topped up with olive oil, flavoured with herb sprigs. Why not drain off 2 tablespoons of this oil to add flavour to the salad – and use the herb sprigs for garnish? To test an avocado for ripeness, press it gently at the stalk end – it should "give" a little.

LEEK AND HAM LAYER

Wrap lightly cooked leeks in roast ham, top with lasagne sheets and a tasty cheese sauce, then bake in the oven until golden and delicious.

SERVES 2

Suitable for freezing

Leeks, *4, trimmed*

Roast ham, *4 slices*

Salt and freshly ground black pepper

Lasagne sheets, *2 (the kind that need no pre-cooking)*

Butter, *25g (1oz)*

Plain flour, *25g (1oz)*

Milk, *300ml (½ pint)*

English mustard, *1 teaspoon*

Mature Cheddar cheese, *75g (3oz), grated*

Oregano or basil leaves, *to garnish*

1   Preheat the oven to 190°C/375°F/Gas 5. Choose a baking dish large enough for the leeks to fit into it in a single layer.
2   Cook the leeks in simmering, lightly salted water for about 4–5 minutes. Drain thoroughly and cool for a few moments.
3   Wrap each leek in a slice of ham and arrange in the baking dish. Season with a little salt and pepper, then place the lasagne sheets on top.
4   To make the cheese sauce, put the butter, flour and milk into a saucepan and bring up to the boil, stirring constantly with a wire whisk until thickened and smooth. Remove from the heat and add the mustard and most of the cheese. Stir well, season with salt and pepper and

pour evenly over the lasagne sheets. Sprinkle the reserved cheese on top.
5   Bake in the oven for 35–40 minutes, until bubbling and golden brown. Serve, garnished with oregano or basil leaves.

COOK'S TIP:

▓ Try this dish another time without the lasagne, and bake for just 20 minutes.

SPAGHETTI CARBONARA

Enjoy this classic pasta dish of eggs, pancetta or smoked bacon with single cream and grated cheese – it's simply delicious.

SERVES 4

Butter, *50g (2oz)*

Pancetta or smoked bacon, *110g (4oz), snipped into pieces*

Garlic clove, *1, crushed*

Spaghetti or tagliatelle, *300g (11oz)*

Eggs, *4*

Single cream, *150ml (¼ pint)*

Mature Cheddar cheese, *75g (3oz) finely grated*

Flat-leaf parsley, *1 tablespoon, chopped*

Salt and freshly ground black pepper

1   Melt half the butter in a frying pan and add the pancetta or smoked bacon. Fry gently for about 5 minutes, then add the crushed garlic and cook for 2–3 more minutes.
2   Meanwhile, cook the spaghetti or tagliatelle in plenty of boiling, lightly salted water for about 8 minutes – or according to pack instructions – until just cooked.
3   Beat together the eggs, single cream and 50g (2oz) of the cheese. Add the parsley and season with salt and pepper.
4   Drain the spaghetti or tagliatelle and return it to the saucepan with the remaining butter. Add the cream mixture and pancetta or bacon, then cook over a low heat, stirring, for 1–2 minutes. Serve, sprinkled with the remaining cheese.

COOK'S TIP:

▓ Look for pancetta in the chill cabinet at the supermarket – where you can often find it in small packs, already chopped. Otherwise, try buying it from a delicatessen.

ITALIAN PARMA HAM AND PASTA PLATTER

Capture the best of Italian flavours in this wonderful salad – perfect for casual entertaining.

SERVES 4

Pasta shapes, *50g (2oz)*

Plum or ordinary tomatoes, *6, sliced*

Parma ham, *12 thin slices*

Cheshire or Wensleydale cheese, *110g (4oz), crumbled*

Baby plum or cherry tomatoes, *12, halved*

Onion, *1 small, thinly sliced*

Cucumber, *10cm (4 inch) piece, finely chopped*

Olives, *75g (3oz)*

Olive oil, *3 tablespoons*

Lemon juice, *2 tablespoons*

Salt and freshly ground black pepper

Oregano or basil leaves and lemon wedges, *to garnish*

1 Cook the pasta shapes in plenty of lightly salted boiling water for 8–10 minutes, or according to pack instructions, until just tender.

2 Meanwhile, arrange the sliced tomatoes on a large serving platter and top with folds of Parma ham. Sprinkle with the crumbled cheese, then top with the baby plum or cherry tomatoes, onion, cucumber and olives.

3 Whisk the olive oil and lemon juice in a large bowl and season with salt and pepper. Drain the cooked pasta and add to the bowl, tossing to coat in the mixture. Allow to cool, then spoon over the salad.

4 Garnish with oregano or basil leaves and lemon wedges, then serve.

COOK'S TIP:

■ If you want to prepare the salad in advance, cover it with cling film and keep it chilled, though allow 20 minutes or so for it to reach room temperature before you serve it, to appreciate the flavours.

PASTA AND VEGETABLE FRITTATA

A frittata is a thick omelette, best served warm rather than piping hot. It's similar to Spanish tortilla, though this version uses cooked pasta and more vegetables.

SERVES 4

Suitable for vegetarians • Suitable for freezing

Small pasta shapes, *75g (3oz)*	
Butter, *25g (1oz)*	
Spring onions, *1 bunch, trimmed and finely chopped*	
Garlic clove, *1, crushed*	
Red pepper, *1, deseeded and sliced*	
Courgette, *1, sliced*	
Eggs, *4, beaten*	
Milk, *4 tablespoons*	
Lancashire cheese, *75g (3oz), crumbled or grated*	
Mixed dried herbs, *1 teaspoon*	
Salt and freshly ground black pepper	

1 Cook the pasta shapes in lightly salted boiling water for about 8–10 minutes, or according to pack instructions. Drain, rinse with cold water and drain well.

2 Melt the butter in a large frying pan and cook the spring onions and garlic gently for about 3 minutes, then add the red pepper and courgette. Cook over a low heat for about 10 minutes, stirring occasionally, until all the vegetables are tender.

3 Beat the eggs and milk together, add the pasta, cheese and dried herbs, then season with salt and pepper. Pour into the pan and cook over a medium low heat until set. Brown the top under a medium hot grill.

4 Allow the frittata to cool for a few minutes, then serve alone or with a simple green salad.

COOK'S TIP:

▓ This frittata is very tasty served cold for picnics and packed lunches. Cut it into wedges and pack in a polythene box for easy transportation.

MINESTRONE WITH SOURED CREAM AND CRISPY BACON

This fantastic meal-in-a-bowl soup is packed with chunky fresh vegetables, with quick-cook macaroni to make it more substantial.

SERVES 4 – 6

Suitable for freezing

Butter, *25g (1oz)*

Streaky bacon, *2 rashers, snipped into small pieces*

Onion, *1, chopped*

Celery, *2 sticks, sliced*

Swede or turnip, *225g (8oz), cut into chunks*

Carrots, *2, chopped*

Chopped tomatoes, *1 x 400g can*

Vegetable stock cubes, *2, dissolved in 900ml (1½ pints) hot water*

Italian mixed dried herbs, *2 teaspoons*

Quick-cook macaroni, *50g (2oz)*

Salt and freshly ground black pepper

Soured cream, *4–6 tablespoons, to serve*

Parsley sprigs, *to garnish (optional)*

1 Melt the butter in a very large saucepan and fry the bacon bits until brown and crispy. Lift them out with a draining spoon and set to one side on sheets of kitchen paper.

2 Add the onion, celery, swede or turnip and carrots to the saucepan and cook for a few minutes, stirring often.

3 Tip the tomatoes into the saucepan and add the vegetable stock and dried herbs. Bring up to the boil, then reduce the heat to low. Cover and simmer gently for about 20 minutes, until the vegetables are tender.

4 Add the macaroni and cook for about 5 minutes, or according to pack instructions, until tender. Taste the soup and season with salt and pepper.

5 Ladle the minestrone into warmed bowls and serve at once, topped with soured cream and sprinkled with the crispy bacon bits and a little extra black pepper. Garnish with parsley sprigs, if you like.

COOK'S TIP:

▪ If you prefer a thinner soup – or you want to spin it out to feed more people – add one more can of chopped tomatoes and another 300ml (½ pint) of vegetable stock.

AUBERGINE, MUSHROOM AND TOMATO BOLOGNAISE

Try this delicious pasta dish – it's a cheap and nutritious vegetarian version of a meat bolognaise.

SERVES 4

Suitable for vegetarians • Suitable for freezing

Butter, *40g (1½oz)*

Olive oil, *2 tablespoons*

Onion, *1, chopped*

Garlic cloves, *2, crushed*

Aubergine, *1 large, finely chopped*

Mushrooms, *175g (6oz), sliced*

Passata (sieved tomato sauce), *300ml (½ pint)*

Tomatoes, *3 large, skinned and chopped*

Vegetable stock cube, *1*

Italian mixed dried herbs, *2 teaspoons*

Dark or light muscovado sugar, *1 teaspoon*

Salt and freshly ground black pepper

Linguine or spaghetti, *300g (11oz)*

Fresh herb sprigs, *to garnish*

Mature Cheddar cheese, *finely grated, to serve*

1 Heat 25g (1oz) of the butter in a large saucepan with the olive oil. Add the onion and garlic, stir well, then cover and reduce the heat to low. Allow them to "sweat" for 4–5 minutes.

2 Add the aubergine and mushrooms to the saucepan. Stir well, cover and cook over a very low heat for a further 5 minutes.

3 Pour the passata into the saucepan and add the tomatoes, stock cube, herbs and sugar. Season with salt and pepper, then cook, uncovered, for about 20–30 minutes, until reduced and thickened.

4 About 15 minutes before you want to eat, cook the linguine or spaghetti in plenty of lightly salted boiling water until just tender, according to pack instructions. Drain well, then stir through the remaining butter.

5 Divide the pasta between 4 warmed plates and top with the bolognaise sauce. Garnish with fresh herb sprigs and serve with the grated Cheddar.

COOK'S TIP:

▓ Do make sure that you chop the aubergine finely, so that it cooks down to give the sauce "body". The sugar brings out the taste of the tomatoes, and gives a richness and depth of flavour.

SUMMER VEGETABLE PASTA

A perfect pasta bake for lovers of fresh vegetables, this recipe is easy, delicious and very nutritious.

SERVES 4

Suitable for vegetarians • Suitable for freezing

Pasta shapes, *175g (6oz)*

Butter, *50g (2oz)*

Red onion, *1, sliced*

Garlic clove, *1, crushed*

Sun-dried tomatoes in olive oil, *50g (2oz) drained and chopped*

Button mushrooms, *150g (5oz), wiped and sliced*

Courgette, *1, sliced*

Baby corn, *110g (4oz), sliced in half*

Tomato pasta sauce, *1 x 275g jar*

Eggs, *2*

Greek-style natural yogurt, *300g (11oz)*

Mature Cheddar cheese, *150g (5oz), grated*

Basil or oregano, *1 tablespoon, chopped, plus sprigs to garnish*

Salt and freshly ground black pepper

1 Preheat the oven to 200°C/400°F/Gas 6.
2 Cook the pasta shapes in plenty of boiling, lightly salted water until just tender, about 8–10 minutes, or according to pack instructions.
3 Meanwhile, melt the butter in a large frying pan and sauté the onion and garlic gently for 5 minutes. Add the sun-dried tomatoes and all the remaining vegetables and cook for 5 more minutes, stirring frequently.
4 Drain the pasta well and add to the vegetable mixture with the pasta sauce, stirring to combine. Transfer to a large buttered ovenproof dish.
5 Beat together the eggs and yogurt, then stir in the cheese. Add the basil or oregano and season well with salt and freshly ground black pepper. Pour evenly over the pasta and vegetables. Bake for 20–25 minutes until set and golden brown. Serve, garnished with fresh herb sprigs.

COOK'S TIP:

■ You could use other regional British cheeses in this pasta bake as a change from Cheddar – try Red Leicester or Double Gloucester instead.

QUICK PRAWN AND CRAB SUPPER

A seafood pasta dish that has been inspired by Thai flavours – making it very tasty indeed.

SERVES 4 AS A STARTER OR 2 FOR A MAIN MEAL

Pasta shells, *150g (5oz)*

Butter, *40g (1½oz)*

Garlic clove, *1, crushed*

Baby leeks, *6, sliced (or use 2 ordinary leeks)*

Root ginger, *1 teaspoon, peeled and finely shredded*

Fresh green chilli, *1, deseeded and finely chopped*

Prawns, *350g (12oz), defrosted if frozen*

Crab, *1 x 200g (7oz) can, drained*

Light soy sauce, *1–2 tablespoons*

Salt and freshly ground black pepper

1   Cook the pasta shells in plenty of lightly salted boiling water for 8–10 minutes, or according to pack instructions, until just tender.

2   Meanwhile, melt the butter in a frying pan or wok and sauté the garlic and leeks for about 5–6 minutes, until softened and tender.

3   Add the ginger and chilli to the frying pan or wok and cook for another 2 minutes. Stir in the prawns and crab and cook for another few moments to heat them through.

4   Drain the cooked pasta well, then return to the saucepan and add the crab and prawn mixture. Season to taste with soy sauce, salt and pepper, heat for a few moments, then divide between warmed serving plates.

COOK'S TIP:

■   Chopped fresh coriander tastes fabulous sprinkled over the finished dish.

SPINACH AND SOFT CHEESE CANNELLONI

Vegetarians will love this tasty pasta bake – and so will everyone else.

SERVES 4

Suitable for vegetarians • Suitable for freezing

Onion, *1, halved*

Celery stick, *1, roughly chopped*

Bay leaf, *1*

Milk, *300ml (½ pint)*

Spinach, *450g (1lb)*

Chopped tomatoes, *1 x 400g can*

Italian dried mixed herbs, *1 teaspoon*

Cannelloni tubes, *16 (the kind that need no pre-cooking)*

Low-fat soft cheese, *3 x 200g (7oz) tubs*

Butter, *25g (1oz)*

Plain flour, *25g (1oz)*

Salt and freshly ground black pepper

1 Put the onion, celery, bay leaf and milk into a saucepan. Bring up to the boil, then remove from the heat and allow to infuse for 10–15 minutes, then strain the milk into a jug. Keep the onion and celery to one side.

2 Cook the spinach in a very small amount of water for 3–4 minutes, until the leaves wilt. Drain well, squeezing out the excess moisture. Spread it over the base of a large baking dish.

3 Chop the onion and celery used for infusing the milk and put them into a saucepan with the tomatoes and dried herbs. Simmer for about 5 minutes until reduced slightly. Spread over the top of the spinach.

4 Stuff the cannelloni tubes with the low-fat soft cheese and arrange them on top of the tomato mixture, in a single layer if possible.

5 Preheat the oven to 190°C/375°F/Gas 5.

6 Put the butter, flour and cooled milk into a saucepan and bring up to the boil, stirring constantly with a wire whisk until thickened and smooth. Season with salt and pepper, then pour evenly over the cannelloni. Bake for about 25 minutes, until bubbling and golden brown.

COOK'S TIP:

■ Use frozen leaf spinach if you like, cooking it lightly first, following pack instructions.

MANGO, MELON AND CHICKEN PASTA SALAD

This fruity chicken salad is a real winner. It makes a delicious lunch or light meal in the summer months.

SERVES 4 AS A STARTER OR 2 FOR A MAIN MEAL

Pasta shapes, *110g (4oz)*

Root ginger, *1 teaspoon, peeled and finely grated*

Clear honey, *1 tablespoon*

Fresh soured cream or Greek-style natural yogurt, *150ml (5fl oz)*

Cooked chicken, *350g (12oz), chopped*

Salt and freshly ground black pepper

Charentais or cantaloupe melon, *225g (8oz), chopped*

Mango, *1, peeled, stoned and chopped*

Mixed salad leaves, *a handful*

Cucumber, *5cm (2 inch) piece, finely chopped*

1　Cook the pasta shapes in plenty of lightly salted boiling water for 8–10 minutes, or according to pack instructions, until just tender.

2　Meanwhile, mix together the ginger, honey and soured cream or yogurt in a large bowl.

3　Drain the cooked pasta and rinse in cold water to cool quickly. Drain well, then add to the creamy dressing with the chicken, tossing the ingredients together. Season with salt and pepper.

4　Mix together the melon, mango and salad leaves, then spoon onto serving plates with the chicken mixture. Season with a little extra ground black pepper, sprinkle with chopped cucumber and serve at once.

COOK'S TIP:

▪ The soured cream or yogurt mixture makes a fabulous accompaniment to a large wedge of melon, so do try it another time.

SALAMI, LEMON AND ASPARAGUS PASTA

Toss papardelle or tagliatelle – Italian pasta noodles – with butter, peas, grated lemon zest, crème fraîche, asparagus and thin strips of salami. Finish off with finely grated mature Cheddar for a simply delicious dish.

SERVES 4

Papardelle or tagliatelle, *300g (11oz)*

Asparagus, *110g (4oz), cut into short lengths*

Butter, *25g (1oz)*

Frozen petit pois or garden peas, *110g (4oz)*

Crème fraîche or soured cream, *300ml (10fl oz)*

Milk, *4 tablespoons*

Lemon zest, *½ teaspoon, + extra, to garnish*

Mature Cheddar cheese, *50g (2oz), finely grated*

Mint or basil, *1 tablespoon, chopped*

Salt and freshly ground black pepper

Salami, *110g (4oz) cut into strips*

1 Cook the papardelle or tagliatelle in plenty of boiling, lightly salted water for about 10–12 minutes, or according to pack instructions, until just tender. At the same time, cook the asparagus in a little lightly salted water for about 4–5 minutes, until just tender, then drain well.

2 Meanwhile, melt the butter in a saucepan and add the peas, then stir in the crème fraîche or soured cream, milk, lemon zest, most of the grated Cheddar and the chopped herbs. Heat gently, stirring, for about 3 minutes. Season with salt and pepper.

3 Drain the pasta well, then return it to the saucepan and add the sauce, asparagus and salami, stirring gently to mix. Reheat for a few moments, then divide between 4 warmed plates and serve at once, garnished with the reserved cheese and fine shreds of lemon zest.

COOK'S TIP:

▧ Use unwaxed lemons if possible, otherwise just scrub ordinary ones thoroughly before grating the zest. Remember to use only the yellow part – the white pith has a bitter flavour and will spoil the taste of the dish.

vegetarian

One creamy mouthful of Mushroom and Tarragon Risotto, and – vegetarian or not – you'll be hooked on these recipes. In fact, more and more people are eating vegetarian food, regardless of whether they eat meat, fish and poultry at other times. So think of these recipes as being food for everyone, to be enjoyed in its own right.

In this chapter you'll find some really fresh, tasty ideas that are suitable for many different occasions. There's delicious Wensleydale Roasted Vegetable Tart, for instance – perfect for a summer meal, picnic or buffet. Or try the easy Quick Cauliflower and Potato Curry – full of flavour, and so good for you. For our health's sake it's a great idea to eat more vegetables, and the recipes here will give you the know-how.

Getting the hang of...

Risotto is a classic Italian dish that has become increasingly popular in this country over the last few years. You can make it with many different ingredients, though you are aiming for a soft, creamy texture with flavours that marry, not clash.

In this recipe, the risotto rice is cooked with white wine to give it an excellent flavour, though you could just use extra stock instead of wine if you'd rather. Use well-flavoured stock cubes, or make your own vegetable stock if you have the time. Add it little by little to the rice, allowing each addition to be absorbed before adding the next. Risotto is not difficult to make, though it does require a little patience.

When the rice is tender, just before you are ready to serve, you can let the risotto "catch" slightly on the bottom of the pan to form a crust. This tastes delicious — though you must be careful not to burn it.

MUSHROOM AND TARRAGON RISOTTO

The secret of a successful risotto is simple — use the correct type of rice. Look out for arborio or carnaroli rice, sometimes just referred to as risotto rice. This will absorb all the wonderful flavours to become soft and mellow, yet it will still retain its shape.

SERVES 6

Suitable for vegetarians

Butter, *50g (2oz)*	
Olive oil, *1 tablespoon*	
Risotto rice, *500g (1lb 2oz)*	
Onion, *1 large, chopped*	
Red pepper, *1 large, deseeded and chopped*	
Dry white wine, *200ml (⅓ pint)*	
Vegetable stock cubes, *2, dissolved in 1.2 litres (2 pints) of hot water*	
Lemon, *1*	
Fine green beans, *75g (3oz), trimmed and chopped*	
Mushrooms, *350g (12oz), sliced*	
Tarragon sprigs, *a few (or 1 tsp dried) + extra, for garnish*	
Lancashire cheese, *110g (4oz), grated or crumbled*	
Salt and freshly ground black pepper	

1 In a very large frying pan or saucepan, heat the butter and olive oil together. Add the rice and sauté gently until it looks translucent, about 5 minutes. Add the onion and pepper and cook for a few more minutes.

2 Add the wine to the rice and cook gently until it has been absorbed, stirring frequently.

3 Add about one quarter of the stock to the rice, stir and allow it to simmer gently.

4 Pare the zest from the lemon using a potato peeler or sharp knife, and add it to the rice with 2 tablespoons of lemon juice, then add the green beans, mushrooms and tarragon. Add further stock to the rice, as needed, to keep it moist. Stir from time to time until it is tender — it will take about 20–25 minutes to cook.

5 Add the Lancashire cheese, season to taste with salt and pepper, stir well and serve, garnished with fresh herb sprigs.

COOK'S TIP:

▪ A couple of tablespoons of single cream stirred into the risotto just before serving will add extra creaminess.

COTSWOLD POTATO AND PARSNIP BAKE

Cotswold cheese is Double Gloucester with chives and onion – and it has a fabulous flavour. Here it is layered with sliced potatoes and parsnips to make a tasty vegetarian bake.

SERVES 4

Suitable for vegetarians

Potatoes, *1.5kg (3lb 5oz), cut into chunks*	
Parsnips, *2 large, thinly sliced*	
Butter, *15g (½oz)*	
Salt and freshly ground black pepper	
Cotswold cheese, *225g (8oz), grated*	
Eggs, *2, beaten*	
Single cream or milk, *300ml (½ pint)*	

1 Preheat the oven to 190°C/375°F/Gas 5.
2 Par-boil the potatoes and parsnips in lightly salted water for about 10 minutes. Drain, cool slightly, then slice the potatoes.
3 Butter a large baking dish and layer in half the potatoes and parsnips, seasoning as you go with salt and pepper. Scatter half the grated cheese on top, then layer the remaining potatoes and parsnips in the baking dish.

4 Beat together the eggs and single cream or milk and pour into the dish. Scatter the remaining cheese over the surface and bake for approximately 35–45 minutes, until the vegetables are tender and the topping is brown.

COOK'S TIP:

■ If you can't find Cotswold cheese use regular Double Gloucester and add 6 very finely chopped spring onions to the cheese layers.

GLOUCESTER VEGETABLE OMELETTE

Never forget the appeal of freshly cooked omelettes. They're quick, nutritious and they taste terrific.

SERVES 2

Suitable for vegetarians

Stir-fry vegetables (fresh or frozen), *225g (8oz)*	
Eggs, *4*	
Milk, *4 tablespoons*	
Salt and freshly ground black pepper	
Butter, *15g (½oz)*	
Double Gloucester or Cheddar cheese, *50g (2oz), grated*	

1 Cook the stir-fry vegetables in a little lightly salted water for about 3 minutes, until just tender. Drain well and keep hot.
2 Beat the eggs and milk together. Season with a little salt and pepper.
3 Heat half the butter in an omelette pan until just beginning to foam. Pour in half the egg mixture, and cook over a medium-high heat until the base sets. Using a wooden spatula, push the cooked egg towards the middle of the pan, so that the raw egg flows over the surface, enabling it to set.
4 Scatter the omelette with half the cheese and allow it to melt for a moment or two. Spoon half the vegetables on top, then fold over and lift out onto a warm plate. Keep in a warm place whilst you cook the second omelette.

COOK'S TIP:

■ This omelette is very good for you. It provides protein – essential for growth and repair of body tissues – along with vitamins A, C, D, E and K, as well as iron.

MELTING SOMERSET BRIE WITH GRILLED VEGETABLES

Grilled vegetables are so delicious, and they're even better when topped with slices of melting Somerset brie.

SERVES 4

Suitable for vegetarians

Peppers, *1 yellow, 1 red, halved and deseeded*

Butter, *25g (1oz)*

Olive oil, *4 tablespoons*

Aubergine, *1 medium, sliced*

Focaccia or ciabatta bread, *4 slices*

Sun-dried tomato paste or purée, *2 tablespoons*

Somerset brie, *225g (8oz), sliced*

Red wine vinegar, *2 tablespoons*

Salt and freshly ground black pepper

Pitted black olives, *about 12, thinly sliced (optional)*

Fresh herb sprigs, *to garnish*

1   Preheat the grill. Put the peppers, skin side up, on to the grill rack. Grill until the skins blacken and char. Switch off the grill and shut its door, leaving the peppers to cool in the steamy atmosphere. Leave them for about 15 minutes, then you will be able to peel off the skins easily.

2   Meanwhile, heat the butter and 1 tablespoon of olive oil in a frying pan. Add the aubergine slices and cook gently, turning once, until browned and softened.

3   Toast the bread, spread with the sun-dried tomato paste or purée, then arrange the aubergine slices on top. Tear the skinned peppers into large pieces and pile on to the aubergines, then finish off with slices of Somerset brie. Grill under a medium heat until the cheese starts to brown and melt.

4   Whisk the remaining olive oil with the wine vinegar. Season with salt and pepper and spoon over the cheese. Scatter with sliced olives, if using, and garnish with fresh herb sprigs.

COOK'S TIP:

▪ Make this tasty recipe with large mushrooms and tomatoes if you're not keen on peppers and aubergines.

MARROW STUFFED WITH ROASTED VEGETABLES

A delicious vegetarian recipe that makes a main course for two, or serves four for a lighter meal.

SERVES 2–4

Suitable for vegetarians

Leek, *1, trimmed and sliced*

Butternut squash or sweet potato, *110g (4oz), cubed*

Red onion, *1 small, chopped*

Fennel, *1 small bulb, sliced*

Garlic cloves, *1–2, thinly sliced*

Cumin seeds, *½ teaspoon*

Coriander seeds, *½ teaspoon, lightly crushed (optional)*

Olive oil, *2–3 tablespoons*

Salt and freshly ground black pepper

Double Gloucester or Cheddar cheese, *75g (3oz)*

Fresh breadcrumbs, *50g (2oz)*

Marrow, *1 medium, halved lengthways and deseeded*

1   Preheat the oven to 200°C/400°F/Gas 6.

2   Put all the vegetables, apart from the marrow, into a roasting tin. Sprinkle with the garlic, cumin, coriander (if using) and olive oil and season with salt and pepper. Toss together, then transfer to the oven and roast for 20 minutes, turning the vegetables over after 10 minutes.

3   Grate half the cheese and cut the remainder into small cubes. Mix the grated cheese with the breadcrumbs.

4   Arrange the marrow halves in a baking dish or roasting tin, cut side up. Sprinkle the insides with about two-thirds of the breadcrumb mixture. Spoon the roasted vegetables on top, then cover with foil and return to the oven to bake for another 30 minutes.

5   Remove the foil and scatter the cheese cubes and remaining breadcrumb mixture over the marrow. Return to the oven – uncovered – and bake for another 10–15 minutes.

COOK'S TIP:

▧ Vary the vegetables according to your preferences or whatever is in season.

CHEESE, TOMATO AND SPINACH STACK

This pancake stack is layered with pasta sauce, sliced tomatoes, freshly cooked spinach and grated Cheddar or Wensleydale. It's rather like a vegetarian lasagne – and it tastes fantastic.

SERVES 4–6

Suitable for vegetarians
Suitable for freezing

Plain flour, *175g (6oz)*

Eggs, *2 small*

Milk, *450ml (¾ pint)*

Vegetable oil, *1 tablespoon*

Spinach, *350g (12oz)*

Sun-dried tomato paste, *4 tablespoons*

Pasta sauce, *1 x 350g (12oz) jar*

Tomatoes, *5, thinly sliced*

Cheddar or Wensleydale cheese, *175g (6oz), grated*

Salt and freshly ground black pepper

1 Tip the flour into a large bowl and add a generous pinch of salt. Add the eggs and milk and beat together using a hand whisk to make a smooth batter. Allow to stand for a few minutes.

2 Heat a heavy-based pancake pan, adding a few drops of vegetable oil. Pour in some batter, tilting the pan around to make a thin pancake. Cook over a medium heat, and when it has set on the surface, flip over to cook the other side. Cool on sheets of kitchen paper. Continue to make six or seven pancakes in this way until all the batter is used up.

3 Pack the spinach into a large saucepan and add a little water. Cover and cook for about 3–4 minutes until the spinach has wilted. Drain well, squeezing out any surplus moisture.

4 Preheat the oven to 180°C/350°F/Gas 4.

5 Stack the pancakes on a lightly greased baking sheet, spreading alternate layers with sun-dried tomato paste and spinach, and the next with pasta sauce, sliced tomatoes and cheese. Season each layer with a little salt and pepper.

6 Transfer to the oven and bake until heated through – about 25–30 minutes. Cool for about 4–5 minutes, then slice into generous wedges.

COOK'S TIP:

▓ Any variety of pasta sauce will work well in this recipe – tomato with herbs, peppers, onion and garlic or olives – just choose the one you prefer.

RISOTTO-STUFFED VEGETABLES

Vegetarian food is never dull – especially when you serve these colourful risotto-filled peppers and tomatoes.

SERVES 4

Suitable for vegetarians

Butter, *25g (1oz)*

Risotto rice, *150g (5oz)*

Baby leeks, shallots or small onions, *2, chopped*

Dry white wine, *150ml (¼ pint)*

Vegetable stock, *600ml (1 pint)*

Button mushrooms, *110g (4oz), wiped and sliced*

Courgette, *1 small, chopped*

Mature Cheddar cheese, *50g (2oz), finely grated*

Salt and freshly ground black pepper

Large tomatoes, *4, halved*

Red, yellow or green peppers, *4, halved and deseeded*

1 Heat the butter in a large frying pan and sauté the rice gently for 3–4 minutes. Add the leeks, shallots or onions and cook for 2–3 more minutes, without browning.
2 Pour in the wine and bubble up for a few moments. Add about a quarter of the stock, bring up to simmering point and cook until it has been absorbed. Add the remaining stock a little at a time, cooking gently until the rice is swollen and tender – this will take about 20 minutes. Stir occasionally, adding more stock or water if needed.
3 Preheat the oven to 190°C/375°F/Gas 5.
4 Mix the cooked rice with the mushrooms and courgette. Stir in the cheese, then season to taste.
5 Slice the tops from the tomatoes and scoop out the seeds. Arrange with the pepper halves in a greased roasting tin. Fill with the rice mixture, popping the tops back onto the tomatoes. Bake for about 20–25 minutes, until the vegetables are tender.

COOK'S TIPS:

▧ Try aubergines as an alternative to peppers and tomatoes, scooping out some of the flesh.

▧ If there's too much risotto mixture, just keep it to one side to serve with the vegetables when they are cooked.

WEST COUNTRY CHEDDAR, ONION AND TOMATO TARTS

Chilled or frozen filo pastry is so easy to use. Try it in this recipe for delicious savoury tarts – perfect for a light lunch, snack or special starter.

SERVES 6

Suitable for vegetarians

Butter, *110g (4oz)*

Filo pastry sheets, *6 (approx. 225g/8oz), defrosted if frozen*

Red onions, *2, sliced*

Garlic clove, *1, crushed*

Plum tomatoes, *6, skinned, deseeded and sliced*

Sun-dried tomato paste, *2 tablespoons*

Wine vinegar, *2 teaspoons*

Dark muscovado sugar, *2 teaspoons*

Salt and freshly ground black pepper

Cheddar cheese, *50g (2oz), grated*

Thyme, basil or parsley sprigs, *to garnish*

1 Preheat the oven to 200°C/400°F/Gas 6.

2 Melt 75g (3oz) of the butter. Unfold the sheets of filo pastry and brush each one with melted butter, stacking them on top of each other.

Cut the pastry into six piles, measuring approximately 10cm (4 inches) square. Layer these buttered filo squares into 6 individual tartlet tins. Bake for 8–10 minutes until golden brown.

3 Meanwhile, melt the remaining butter in a frying pan and gently fry the onions and garlic for about 5–6 minutes. Add the tomatoes and cook for another 2–3 minutes, stirring occasionally. Stir in the tomato paste, vinegar and sugar and cook gently for another few moments, then season to taste.

4 Sprinkle an equal amount of cheese into each filo tart, then pile the warm tomato mixture on top. Garnish with a few sprigs of thyme, basil or parsley, then serve.

COOK'S TIP:

▨ Sun-dried tomato paste adds a delicious intensity of flavour, but if you can't find it, use sun-dried or ordinary tomato purée.

CARROT AND FENNEL BAKE WITH CHESHIRE TOPPING

Fennel is a delicious vegetable, so we should perhaps use it more often. Serve this tasty dish with crusty fresh bread to mop up the juices.

SERVES 4

Suitable for vegetarians

Fennel, *4 bulbs*	
Lemon juice, *2 tablespoons*	
Butter, *25g (1oz)*	
Carrots, *8 small, halved lengthways*	
Red onion, *1, sliced*	
Vegetable stock cube, *1*	
Dried thyme or rosemary, *1 teaspoon*	
Salt and freshly ground black pepper	
Cheshire cheese, *75g (3oz), crumbled or grated*	

1 Preheat the oven to 180°C/350°F/Gas 4.

2 Trim the roots and tops from the fennel and remove the outer leaves, if necessary. Slice each bulb in half, through the root. Put into a saucepan, cover with boiling water and add the lemon juice. Simmer for 5 minutes, then drain well, reserving the liquid.

3 Transfer the fennel to a buttered baking dish. Add the carrots and red onion. Dissolve the stock cube in 300ml (½ pint) of the reserved liquid and pour into the baking dish.

4 Sprinkle the vegetables with the thyme or rosemary. Season with salt and pepper, then dot the remaining butter over the surface. Cover and bake for 35–40 minutes, or until the vegetables are tender.

5 Remove the cover from the vegetables and scatter the surface with the cheese. Return to the oven and bake, uncovered, for another 10–15 minutes.

COOK'S TIP:

■ Celery hearts would make an excellent alternative to fennel. Use two heads of celery for four people, remove the outer sticks and slice the hearts in half.

CELERY AND APPLE SALAD WITH CHEDDAR CURLS

Make this refreshing salad for lunch or supper with apple, celery and crisp lettuce leaves, topped with flaked almonds and clever Cheddar cheese curls.

SERVES 4

Suitable for vegetarians

Cheddar cheese, *50g (2oz), finely grated*	
Lemon juice, *2 tablespoons*	
Celery, *4 sticks, thinly sliced*	
Apples, *2, cored and chopped or thinly sliced*	
Sultanas or raisins, *25g (1oz)*	
Natural yogurt, *150g (5oz)*	
Toasted flaked almonds, *25g (1oz)*	
Romaine or cos lettuce, *1*	
Salt and freshly ground pink or black peppercorns	

1 First of all, make the Cheddar curls. Preheat a hot grill. Sprinkle small mounds of cheese – about 1 tablespoon each – on to a non-stick baking sheet, allowing plenty of room for them to spread. Grill until melted, bubbling and golden brown. Carefully peel them off one at a time whilst still warm, and wrap loosely around the handle of a wooden spoon to curl them (rather like making brandy snaps). Cool completely.

2 Put the lemon juice into a bowl and add the celery, apples, sultanas or raisins, yogurt and almonds. Stir together gently to coat.

3 Arrange the lettuce leaves onto 4 serving plates and top with the salad mixture. Season with salt and pepper, then top each portion with the Cheddar curls.

COOK'S TIP:

■ You may find it a little tricky to make the Cheddar curls, but you'll soon get the hang of it. Take care not to overcook the cheese – when the mounds have melted they still need to be soft in the middle to lift off the baking tray.

WENSLEYDALE ROASTED VEGETABLE TART

A crumbly cheese pastry encases roasted vegetables in this easy-to-make free-form tart.

SERVES 6

Suitable for vegetarians • Suitable for freezing

Courgette, *1 small, sliced*

Aubergine, *1 small, sliced*

Yellow pepper, *1, deseeded and thickly sliced*

Cherry tomatoes, *8*

Red or white onion, *1 small, sliced*

Olive oil, *3 tablespoons*

Wensleydale cheese, *110g (4oz), crumbled*

Single cream, *6 tablespoons*

Thyme leaves, *1 teaspoon*

Chilli flakes, *a pinch (optional)*

Salt and freshly ground black pepper

Pastry:

Plain flour, *225g (8oz)*

Salt, *½ teaspoon*

Butter, *50g (2oz), chilled and cut into pieces*

White vegetable fat, *50g (2oz), chilled and cut into pieces*

Mature Cheddar cheese, *50g (2oz), grated*

Eggs, *2, beaten*

1 Preheat the oven to 200°C/400°F/Gas 6. Put all the vegetables into a roasting pan, sprinkle with the olive oil and toss to mix. Roast for 20 minutes, turning after 10 minutes. Allow to cool.

2 Meanwhile, make the pastry. Put the flour and salt into a large bowl. Rub in the butter and vegetable fat until the mixture looks like fine breadcrumbs. Stir in the grated Cheddar, then add 2 tablespoons of beaten egg and just enough chilled water to make a soft, but not sticky, dough. Knead for a few moments until smooth, then chill for 10 minutes.

3 Roll out the pastry on a lightly floured surface into a circle with a diameter of about 38cm (15 inches). Transfer to a baking sheet – the pastry will overlap the sheet at this stage. Brush the surface of the pastry with beaten egg.

4 Pile the vegetables onto the pastry – leaving a border of about 10cm (4 inches) around the edge. Sprinkle the Wensleydale cheese over the top. Fold the pastry edge over the vegetables, tucking, overlapping and sealing it to make a free-form tart. Brush the pastry with beaten egg.

5 Beat the remaining egg and single cream with the thyme and chilli flakes (if using). Season with salt and pepper, then carefully pour into the tart.

6 Transfer to the oven and bake for about 25 minutes, until the pastry is crisp and golden and the filling has set. Serve warm or cold.

COOK'S TIP:

■ You can use ready-made pastry if you prefer to take a short cut – or make the pastry in a food processor.

QUICK CAULIFLOWER AND POTATO CURRY

A favourite filler for all the family, this healthy vegetable curry is absolutely delicious. "Raita" is a cooling yogurt and cucumber mixture which makes a perfect accompaniment along with warm naan bread.

SERVES 4

Suitable for vegetarians • Suitable for freezing

Butter, *25g (1oz)*

Onion, *1, sliced*

Garlic clove, *1, crushed*

Potatoes, *500g (1lb 2oz), scrubbed and cut into chunks*

Vegetable stock cubes, *2, dissolved in 1.2 litres (2 pints) hot water*

Red and yellow peppers, *1 of each, deseeded and chopped*

Fine green beans, *110g (4oz), sliced*

Cauliflower, *½ small, broken into florets*

Baby corn, *175g (6oz), sliced*

Balti or medium curry paste, *2–3 tablespoons, according to taste*

Salt and freshly ground black pepper

Naan bread, *to serve*

Raita:

Natural yogurt, *150g (5oz)*

Cucumber, *5cm (2 inch) piece, finely chopped*

Fresh coriander or mint, *1 tablespoon, chopped*

1   Melt the butter in a large saucepan and add the onion. Sauté gently for about 3–4 minutes until softened. Add the garlic and cook for another minute or two.

2   Add the potatoes and vegetable stock. Bring up to the boil, then reduce the heat and cook, covered, for about 10 minutes.

3   Add all the remaining vegetables and cook for another 10–15 minutes. They should be tender yet retain some "bite", apart from the potatoes, which should break down a little to thicken the liquid.

4   Whilst the vegetables are cooking, make the raita by mixing together the yogurt, cucumber and coriander or mint.

5   Stir 2 or 3 tablespoons of the curry paste through the cooked vegetables, according to taste. Season with salt and pepper and cook gently for another few minutes.

6   Meanwhile, warm the naan bread in a toaster, under the grill or in a warm oven. Serve with the vegetable curry, accompanied by the cucumber raita.

COOK'S TIP:

▨   Use courgette or aubergine instead of fine green beans, if you prefer.

RED PEPPER AND ONION ROAST WITH GARLIC BREAD

A colourful vegetable roast that makes a tasty light meal, or can be served as a side dish if you prefer.

SERVES 4

Suitable for vegetarians

Onions, red onions and shallots, *680g (1½lb) in total, peeled*

Cumin seeds, *1 teaspoon (optional)*

Salt and freshly ground black pepper

Olive oil, *2 tablespoons*

Red peppers, *2, deseeded and cut into eighths*

Garlic cloves, *4 small, crushed*

Butter, *50g (2oz), softened*

French bread, *½ stick*

Thyme or parsley sprigs, *a few*

1   Preheat the oven to 190°C/375°F/Gas 5.
2   Cut the onions into quarters or chunks. Leave the shallots whole. Tip them into a roasting pan, season with the cumin seeds (if using), salt and black pepper, then sprinkle with the olive oil, tossing to coat.

3   Roast the onions for 20 minutes, then add the peppers, tossing to mix. Roast for a further 20–25 minutes.
4   Mix the crushed garlic with the softened butter.
5   Split the French bread in half horizontally and spread with the garlic butter. Cut into chunks. Scatter over the onions and peppers. Bake for a further 10 minutes, then serve, sprinkled with thyme or parsley and seasoned with black pepper.

COOK'S TIP:

■ If you like, scatter about 75g (3oz) of grated mature Cheddar cheese over the surface of the garlic bread before you return it to the oven.

WATERCRESS, TOMATO AND CHEESE ROULADE

This roulade makes a lovely addition to a summer spread, or serve it as part of a buffet for a special occasion.

SERVES 4–6

Suitable for vegetarians • Suitable for freezing

Butter, *25g (1oz)*
Watercress, rocket or spinach, *225g (8oz)*
Eggs, *4, separated*
Salt and freshly ground black pepper
Spring onions, *6, trimmed and finely chopped*
Plain flour, *25g (1oz)*
Milk, *200ml (⅓ pint)*
Double Gloucester or Red Leicester cheese, *75g (3oz), grated*
Cream cheese, *110g (4oz)*
Tomatoes, *3, skinned, deseeded and chopped*

1 Preheat the oven to 190°C/375°F/Gas 5. Line a 20 x 30cm (8 x 12 inch) Swiss roll tin with non-stick baking paper. Brush with melted butter.

2 Cook the watercress, rocket or spinach in a small amount of water for about 5 minutes, until wilted. Drain thoroughly, then chop finely, using a food processor if you like. Tip into a large mixing bowl and add the egg yolks. Season with salt and pepper.

3 In a large, grease-free bowl, whisk the egg whites until stiff, then fold them into the watercress mixture using a large metal spoon. Pour into the prepared tin and quickly spread the mixture into the corners. Bake for 10–12 minutes until set and tinged a light golden brown.

4 Meanwhile, melt the butter in a saucepan and sauté the spring onions for 2–3 minutes, until softened. Stir in the flour, then cook gently for 1 minute. Remove from the heat and gradually add the milk, then heat, stirring all the time, until thickened and smooth.

5 Stir the grated cheese, cream cheese and tomatoes into the sauce. Season with salt and pepper.

6 Turn out the baked mixture from the Swiss roll tin onto a large sheet of greaseproof paper. Carefully peel away the lining paper and leave to cool. Spread with the sauce, then roll up from the short end. Chill until ready to serve.

COOK'S TIP:

▪ In some supermarkets you can buy mixed bags of watercress, rocket and spinach – two 120g bags would be ideal for this recipe.

MOROCCAN ORANGE SALAD WITH MINT AND YOGURT DRESSING

Couscous is quick and easy to prepare. Whilst it's soaking, chop and prepare the other ingredients.

SERVES 4

Suitable for vegetarians

Couscous, *175g (6oz)*

Oranges, *2*

Clear honey, *1 tablespoon*

Natural yogurt, *4 tablespoons*

Mint sprigs, *a few, chopped*

Raisins or sultanas, *2 heaped tablespoons*

Red onion, *1 small, finely sliced*

Ready-to-eat dried apricots, *110g (4oz), chopped*

Celery sticks, *2, thinly sliced*

Seedless red or green grapes, *110g (4oz) halved*

Lancashire cheese, *110g (4oz), cut into small cubes*

Lamb's lettuce, watercress, red chard or baby spinach leaves, *a handful*

Salt and freshly ground black pepper

Mint sprigs, *to garnish*

1 Put the couscous into a large bowl and add a generous pinch of salt. Pour over enough boiling water to just cover, then leave to soak for about 15–20 minutes, until swollen and tender.

2 Mix together 1 teaspoon of finely grated orange zest with 2 tablespoons of orange juice. Stir in the honey, yogurt and chopped mint. Peel and segment the remaining orange, removing all the pith.

3 Fluff up the soaked couscous with a fork, then add the orange segments, raisins or sultanas, most of the red onion, apricots, celery, grapes and cheese, tossing well to mix. Stir in the lamb's lettuce, watercress, red chard or baby spinach leaves and season with salt and pepper.

4 Divide the salad between 4 serving plates or bowls, garnish with the reserved red onion and mint sprigs, then serve with the yogurt and mint dressing.

COOK'S TIP:

▓ Try using bulghar wheat (cracked wheat) instead of couscous.

hot puddings

Time for a little (or a lot) of pure indulgence, depending on whether you eat a small or a large portion of these fabulous hot puddings. Just look at the Ginger and Banana Sponge Pudding with Hot Toffee Sauce on page 129. Couldn't you just imagine a spoonful melting in your mouth?

If you want something refreshing, then Strawberry and Clementine Fruit Toasts are quick, simple to make and extremely delicious, or try Hot Tropical Fruit Salad – it's a real winner. There's a classic recipe for Bread and Butter Pudding too – so easy when you follow our foolproof recipe. And when you fancy pancakes, try topping them with real dairy ice cream and hot butterscotch sauce. Pudding lovers, you will not be disappointed!

Getting the hang of...

BREAD AND BUTTER PUDDING

Traditional, homely, and as delicious today as ever it was, bread and butter pudding ranks highly as one of our all-time favourites. So why not make one today?

Bread and butter pudding is a really satisfying dessert. Even better, it's extremely easy to make, requiring little effort to put it together. It's very nutritious and easy to digest too, hence its reputation as a favourite nursery pudding. The ingredients are pretty basic – bread, a little butter, eggs, milk, sugar and dried fruit. In this version some exotic dried fruit is used, though you could simply stick to sultanas or raisins if you prefer.

When making bread and butter pudding, it's a good idea to use bread that's at least a day or two old. That way, the bread soaks up the liquid and becomes deliciously soft and gooey – and it's a brilliant way of using up a loaf that has gone slightly stale.

SERVES 6

Suitable for vegetarians
Suitable for freezing

Butter, *40g (1½oz)*

Bun loaf or white bread, *12 small slices from a 1–2 day-old loaf*

Sultanas or raisins, *25g (1oz)*

Ready-to-eat dried apricots, *25g (1oz), sliced*

Ready-to-eat dried papaya, *25g (1oz), cut into tiny chunks*

Eggs, *3 (medium or large)*

Milk, *600ml (1 pint)*

Single cream, *150ml (¼ pint) + extra, to serve*

Golden caster sugar, *40g (1½oz)*

Vanilla extract, *1 teaspoon*

Nutmeg, freshly grated if possible, *¼ teaspoon*

Lemon zest, *1 teaspoon*

1   Use a small amount of the butter to grease a large baking dish with about a 2 litre (3½ pint) capacity. Spread the remaining butter over the slices of bun loaf or bread. Lay the slices in the dish, overlapping them to fit.
2   Scatter the sultanas or raisins over the bread with the apricots and papaya.

3   Beat the eggs in a large jug or mixing bowl, then add the milk, single cream, sugar and vanilla extract. Allow to stand for a few minutes, stirring once or twice, to dissolve the sugar.
4   Pour the egg and milk mixture all over the bread, and let it soak in for a few moments. Cover with cling film and allow to stand for at least 30 minutes – longer if you want to cook the pudding later.
5   Preheat the oven to 180°C/350°F/Gas 4.
6   Sprinkle the surface of the pudding with the nutmeg and lemon zest. Bake for 30–35 minutes, until puffed up and golden brown. Cool for a few minutes, then serve with single cream.

COOK'S TIPS:

▓   Whole nutmeg that you grate yourself tastes the best. It will keep for ages, and when you grate the amount you need it will be fresh and fragrant.

▓   Apricots and papaya give a different twist to this delicious pudding, though just use more sultanas or raisins if you'd rather keep it traditional.

MARZIPAN PLUM CRUNCH WITH CINNAMON CREAM

The very clever crumble topping is made simply by stirring a muesli-type cereal into melted butter, and mixing it with grated marzipan. The flavour is sensational – and has to be eaten to be believed.

SERVES 4–6

Suitable for vegetarians • Suitable for freezing

Plums, *900g (2lb), halved and pitted*	
Light muscovado sugar, *110g (4oz)*	
Butter, *50g (2oz)*	
Crunchy oat cereal or muesli, *150g (5oz)*	
Marzipan, *50g (2oz), grated*	
Double or whipping cream, *150ml (5fl oz)*	
Ground cinnamon, *¼ teaspoon*	

1 Preheat the oven to 190°C/375°F/Gas 5.
2 Put the plums into a baking dish and scatter 75g (3oz) of the sugar over the surface. Bake for 5 minutes whilst preparing the topping.
3 Melt the butter in a saucepan and remove from the heat, then mix in the cereal or muesli, the remaining sugar and half the amount of grated marzipan. Remove the baking dish from the oven and sprinkle the topping over the plums in an even layer, then scatter the remaining marzipan over the top.

4 Bake for about 15–20 minutes, until the plums are tender and the topping is crunchy and golden brown.
5 Whip the cream until soft peaks form, then fold in the cinnamon. Serve with the plum crunch.

COOK'S TIP:

▓ Muscovado sugar is essential to the success of this recipe – you'll find it in every supermarket. Its naturally rich flavour adds so much more taste – making a luscious syrup as the fruit cooks.

HOT BANANAS IN RUM AND RAISIN SAUCE

Delicious desserts don't have to be complicated or time-consuming in order to taste fantastic. This recipe for pan-cooked bananas proves the point perfectly.

SERVES 4

Suitable for vegetarians

Butter, *50g (2oz)*	
Bananas, *4, thickly sliced*	
Golden syrup, *4 tablespoons*	
Light muscovado sugar, *50g (2oz)*	
Raisins or sultanas, *50g (2oz)*	
Rum or brandy, *3 tablespoons*	
Flaked almonds, *1–2 tablespoons*	

1 Melt the butter in a large frying pan and add the bananas. Cook them for about 1–2 minutes over a medium-high heat, turning them over to brown them lightly – though you must avoid over-cooking them, or else they will go soggy.
2 Add the syrup, sugar and raisins or sultanas to the pan. Cook over a low heat, stirring gently, for a minute or two. Remove the pan from the heat whilst you stir in the rum or brandy, then return to the heat to bubble up the sauce for a moment or two. Scatter with the flaked almonds, then serve at once.

COOK'S TIPS:

▓ Choose slightly under-ripe bananas for this recipe. If they are very ripe they will be a bit too soft when cooked.

▓ Serve the bananas alone, or with cream, dairy ice cream, fromage frais or Greek-style natural yogurt.

STRAWBERRY AND CLEMENTINE FRUIT TOASTS

Choose Italian panettone, French-style brioche or a light fruit bread to make these easy, delicious hot fruit toasts. They're so versatile, you could serve them for a snack, a special breakfast or as a stunning dessert.

SERVES 4

Suitable for vegetarians

Butter, *40g (1½oz), softened*

Vanilla extract, *½ teaspoon*

Panettone, brioche or light fruit bread,
4 thick slices

Clementines or satsumas, *4, peeled and sliced*

Strawberries, *175g (6oz), halved*

Golden caster sugar, *25g (1oz)*

Maple syrup, *to serve*

Clotted cream, dairy ice cream or crème
fraîche, *to serve*

1 Preheat the oven to 200°C/400°F/Gas 6.
2 Mix the butter and vanilla extract together, then spread generously over each slice of panettone, brioche or fruit bread. Arrange on a lightly greased baking sheet and top with the clementines or satsumas and strawberries. Sprinkle with the sugar.
3 Bake for about 4–5 minutes, when the bread should be lightly browned at the edges.
4 Remove from the oven and serve at once, drizzled with a little maple syrup and accompanied by clotted cream, ice cream or crème fraîche.

COOK'S TIPS:

■ You can grill the desserts instead of baking them – just keep a watchful eye on them to make sure that they don't burn.

■ Sprinkle a little ground cinnamon or nutmeg over the fruit before baking.

ORANGE SEMOLINA MERINGUE PUDDINGS

Semolina is a classic milk pudding, so it just had to be included in this dairy cookbook! This one is given a new interpretation – it's topped with refreshing orange slices and golden brown meringue.

SERVES 2

Suitable for vegetarians

Semolina, *40g (1½oz)*

Milk, *450ml (¾ pint)*

Sultanas, *25g (1oz)*

Golden caster sugar, *40g (1½oz)*

Vanilla extract, *½ teaspoon*

Ground nutmeg or cinnamon, *pinch*

Oranges, *2 small*

Eggs, *2, separated*

1 Preheat the oven to 190°C/375°F/Gas 5.
2 Put the semolina into a saucepan and blend in the milk. Heat, stirring, until thickened and smooth. Cook gently for a few more minutes, then remove from the heat.

3 Add the sultanas to the semolina with half the sugar, the vanilla extract, nutmeg or cinnamon and 1 teaspoon of finely grated orange zest. Taste, adding a little extra sugar if you would prefer it to be sweeter. Add the egg yolks. Stir well and divide between 2 individual heatproof dishes. Bake for about 10 minutes, or until just set.

4 Meanwhile, prepare the oranges by removing all the peel and pith with a sharp, serrated knife. Slice into segments, removing all the membrane.

5 Whisk the egg whites in a grease-free bowl until they hold their shape. Add the remaining sugar, then whisk until glossy.

6 Top the baked semolina puddings with the orange segments, then pile the meringue on top. Transfer to the oven and bake for about 5 minutes, until golden brown. Serve at once.

COOK'S TIPS:

▓ Use large heat-resistant teacups if you don't have individual pudding dishes – or just use one larger dish if you prefer.

▓ There are two types of meringue – the soft, marshmallow type which is quickly cooked like this one (and used for Lemon Meringue Pie on page 146 or Key Lime Pie on page 155), and the slow-baked dried-out version for pavlovas and cream-filled meringues (see Summer Fruit Pavlova on page 150). Don't confuse the two!

GINGER AND BANANA SPONGE PUDDING WITH HOT TOFFEE SAUCE

If you ever need a recipe that is the definition of comfort food – this is it! Let it gently steam away while you enjoy the wonderful aromas.

SERVES 6

Suitable for vegetarians • Suitable for freezing

Butter, *110g (4oz) + extra for greasing*

Light muscovado sugar, *110g (4oz)*

Eggs, *2, beaten*

Vanilla extract, *1 teaspoon*

Self-raising flour, *110g (4oz)*

Ground ginger, *½ teaspoon*

Salt, *pinch*

Bananas, *2 medium*

Milk, *2 tablespoons*

Stem ginger in syrup, *4 pieces + 3 tablespoons of the syrup from the jar*

Sauce:

Golden syrup, *4 tablespoons*

Butter, *50g (2oz)*

1 In a large mixing bowl, cream the butter and sugar together until light and fluffy. Gradually beat in the eggs, then stir in the vanilla extract. Sift in the flour, ground ginger and salt, then fold in lightly using a large metal spoon.

2 Using a fork or potato masher, mash the bananas thoroughly, then fold them into the creamed mixture with the milk.

3 Butter a 900ml (1½ pint) pudding basin. Slice the stem ginger and place it in the bottom of the basin with the 3 tablespoons of syrup from the jar. Spoon over the creamed mixture and level the surface. Cover the basin tightly with a piece of buttered foil.

4 Steam the pudding in a steamer or a large saucepan for 2 hours 15 minutes, making sure that the water does not boil dry, and topping up with boiling water as needed.

5 Allow the pudding to cool slightly whilst you make the sauce. Gently heat the syrup and butter together, then simmer for 1 minute. Remove the foil from the pudding, run a knife around the edge to loosen it, then invert onto a large plate. Serve with the sauce.

COOK'S TIPS:

▩ Never allow the steamer or saucepan to boil dry – and always top up with boiling water. If cooking in a saucepan, the water needs to be about one-third of the way up the pudding basin.

▩ To measure syrup, warm a metal spoon in boiling water or over a gas flame so that the syrup slides off easily.

▩ Custard or single cream could be served with the pudding instead of the hot toffee sauce.

ICE CREAM PANCAKES WITH BUTTERSCOTCH SAUCE

This is the kind of recipe where you simply won't be able to resist licking the plates – so perhaps it's best if you don't make it for a dinner party!

SERVES 4 (2 PANCAKES EACH)

Suitable for vegetarians • Suitable for freezing

Plain flour, *110g (4oz)*

Salt, *large pinch*

Egg, *1 large*

Milk, *300ml (½ pint)*

Vegetable oil, *2–3 teaspoons*

Butter, *50g (2oz)*

Golden syrup, *2 tablespoons*

Golden caster or light muscovado sugar, *50g (2oz)*

Dairy vanilla ice cream, *about 8 scoops*

1 Sift the flour and salt into a large bowl. Add the egg and milk and beat with a wire whisk to make a smooth batter.

2 Add a few drops of oil to a small pancake pan or heavy-based frying pan. Pour in a thin stream of batter, tilting the pan so that the batter flows evenly across the surface. Cook over a medium heat until set, then flip over to cook the other side. Cook 8 small pancakes altogether, keeping them in a warm place.

3 Make the sauce by gently heating the butter with the syrup and sugar until melted and smooth, but do not boil, or else it will turn to toffee!

4 Serve two pancakes per person, then top with scoops of ice cream. Drizzle with the hot butterscotch sauce and serve at once.

COOK'S TIPS:

▓ If you like, fill the pancakes with cooked, sweetened apple, then roll up and serve with the ice cream and butterscotch sauce.

▓ Freeze pancakes in a stack, interleaved with pieces of greaseproof paper or freezer wrap, to make defrosting easier.

HOT TROPICAL FRUIT SALAD

A hot fresh fruit salad tastes sensational – just make sure that you only cook the fruits lightly, so that they keep their fabulous colours and flavours.

SERVES 4–6

Suitable for vegetarians

Butter, *50g (2oz)*

Fresh pineapple, *1 small, peeled and cut into chunks*

Bananas, *2, sliced*

Kiwi fruit, *2, peeled and cut into chunks*

Mango, *1, peeled, stoned and sliced*

Plums or nectarines, *2, pitted and sliced*

Clear honey, *4 tablespoons*

Lemon juice, *1 tablespoon*

Rum, *1–2 tablespoons (optional)*

Sesame seeds, *1 teaspoon*

Fresh cream, natural yogurt or fromage frais, *to serve*

1 Melt the butter in a large saucepan or frying pan. When it starts to foam add the pineapple, bananas, kiwi fruit, mango and plums or nectarines. Cook for about 3 minutes, until slightly softened and light golden brown.

2 Spoon the honey and lemon juice into the pan and cook gently for 1–2 minutes. Add the rum, if using, then stir gently to mix and bubble up for a moment or two.

3 Share out the fruit and sprinkle with sesame seeds. Serve with fresh cream, natural yogurt or fromage frais.

COOK'S TIPS:

■ If you don't want to use a fresh pineapple, use a large, well-drained can of pineapple chunks in natural juice.

■ You don't have to use such a variety of fruits – just limit it to two types, and use more of them.

PEACH, PLUM AND BANANA SOUFFLÉ OMELETTE

Soufflé omelettes may sound quite "posh", yet they are quick, easy and impressive.

SERVES 2

Suitable for vegetarians

Peach or nectarine, *1, pitted and sliced*

Plums, *2, pitted and sliced*

Lemon juice, *1 tablespoon*

Golden caster sugar, *25g (1oz)*

Banana, *1*

Eggs, *4, separated*

Vanilla extract, *1 teaspoon*

Butter, *15g (½oz)*

Icing sugar, *1 tablespoon*

1   Put the peach or nectarine and plum slices into a small saucepan. Add the lemon juice and half the caster sugar with 4 tablespoons of cold water. Heat gently until the fruit has softened – about 3–4 minutes. Slice the banana, add to the pan, then turn the heat to very low.

2   In a large grease-free bowl, whisk the egg whites until they hold their shape. In a separate bowl, beat the egg yolks with the remaining caster sugar and vanilla extract, then fold into the egg whites.

3   Preheat the grill. Melt half the butter in a medium non-stick omelette pan or frying pan and add half the egg mixture. Cook until set on the base, then place under the grill for a few moments to set the surface. Fill with half the fruit and flip over. Keep warm whilst you make the second omelette, then serve at once, sprinkled with icing sugar.

COOK'S TIP:

■ For a different filling, try apricot and banana. Simply warm 4 tablespoons of apricot conserve or jam with 2 sliced bananas and add a squeeze of lemon juice.

DOUBLE CHOCOLATE PUDDING

Try this lovely chocolate bread pudding, finished off with an orange-flavoured topping.

SERVES 6

Suitable for vegetarians • Suitable for freezing

Butter, *75g (3oz)*	
Bread, *6 slices from a thin-cut white loaf, crusts removed*	
Plain chocolate, *110g (4oz), broken into pieces*	
Dark or light muscovado sugar, *65g (2½oz)*	
Chocolate milk shake, *300ml (½ pint)*	
Evaporated milk, *1 x 170g can*	
Eggs, *2 large*	
Vanilla extract, *1 teaspoon*	
Thick double cream or crème fraîche, *6 tablespoons*	
Finely grated orange zest, *2 teaspoons*	
Cocoa powder, *for sprinkling*	

1 Grease six individual pudding basins with 2 teaspoons of the butter. Tear the bread into pieces and divide them between the basins.

2 Put the remaining butter into a saucepan with the chocolate and sugar. Cook gently over a very low heat, stirring often, until the chocolate and butter has melted, and the sugar has dissolved. Do not allow the mixture to boil. If the sugar is still a little gritty, just remove the pan from the heat and let it stand for a few minutes. Cool slightly.

3 Whisk the chocolate milk, evaporated milk, eggs and vanilla extract together, then gradually whisk in the chocolate sauce mixture.

4 Strain the mixture into the pudding basins. Press the bread down to make sure that it is covered. Put cling film over the basins and chill for 1–2 hours.

5 Preheat the oven to 180°C/350°F/Gas 4. Remove the cling film from the puddings and bake them until set, about 20–25 minutes. When cooked, let them stand for about 5 minutes before turning them out onto serving plates.

6 Stir half the orange zest into the cream or crème fraîche. Use to top each serving of the pudding, then sprinkle with the remaining orange zest and a little cocoa powder.

COOK'S TIPS:

▧ Make your own chocolate flavoured milk by whisking together 300ml (½ pint) of milk with 2 tablespoons of milk shake mix or drinking chocolate.

▧ If you prefer, bake the pudding in one large dish, with a 1.2 litre (2 pint) capacity. Bake for a few minutes longer, until set.

▧ For a really wicked dessert, why not serve the puddings with hot chocolate sauce? Simply follow the recipe for Hot Choc Dip on page 172.

ENGLISH APPLE TARTE TATIN WITH WHIPPED NUTMEG CREAM

You simply must try this delectable "upside down" apple tart. It's cooked in a heavy-based frying pan or skillet that will withstand oven temperatures. Choose one with a diameter of 20–23cm (8–9 inches).

SERVES 4–6

Suitable for vegetarians

Granulated sugar, *75g (3oz)*

Water, *3 tablespoons*

Butter, *75g (3oz), cut into pieces*

Cox's apples, *6–8, depending on their size*

Ready-rolled puff pastry, *1 sheet, defrosted if frozen*

Double cream, *150ml (¼ pint)*

Freshly ground nutmeg, *generous pinch*

1 Put the sugar and water into a 20–23cm (8–9 inch) frying pan or skillet that will withstand oven temperatures. On the hob, bring the sugar and water to the boil over a high heat, then reduce the temperature and cook over a medium heat, without stirring, until the sugar begins to caramelise, turning a rich amber colour.

2 Remove the pan from the heat and add the butter. Be careful, as the mixture will bubble up quite furiously, but it will soon settle.

3 Peel, quarter and core the apples, then layer them in the pan, cut sides uppermost, until they are almost level with the top of the pan.

4 Return the pan to the hob and cook over a low heat for 15–20 minutes, so that the apples cook in the caramel sauce, making sure that they don't burn. Remove from the heat and cool completely.

5 Preheat the oven to 190°C/375°F/Gas 5.

6 Place the sheet of puff pastry over the frying pan or skillet, and trim around the edge, allowing an overlap of about 1cm (½ inch). Tuck this overlap down the inside of the pan.

7 Place the frying pan or skillet on to a baking sheet and bake for about 20 minutes, until the pastry is risen and golden brown. Allow to cool for about 15 minutes, then loosen the pastry from around the edges. Place a large serving plate over the pan, then hold firmly and invert to release the tart on to the plate.

8 Whip the cream in a chilled bowl until soft peaks form. Fold in the nutmeg and serve with the tarte tatin.

COOK'S TIP:

■ Plums, nectarines or peaches could all be used instead of apples, though you will need to reduce their cooking time on the hob to about 5 minutes.

APPLE AND PLUM TARTS WITH CLOTTED CREAM

These delightful pastries are simplicity itself to make. Serve them just warm with a generous dollop of fresh clotted cream for a heavenly dessert.

MAKES 8

Suitable for vegetarians • Suitable for freezing

Ready-rolled puff pastry sheet, *1 x 375g (13oz), defrosted*

Ground almonds, *110g (4oz)*

Golden caster sugar, *40g (1½oz), plus extra for sprinkling*

Egg, *1 large, beaten*

Plums, *2, halved and pitted*

Eating apple, *1, halved and cored*

Flaked almonds, *25g (1oz)*

Clotted cream or single cream, *8 tablespoons*

1 Preheat the oven to 200°C/400°F/Gas 6. Lightly grease two baking sheets.
2 Unroll the pastry sheet and cut out 8 circles using a 9cm (3½ inch) cutter. Place four circles on to each baking sheet.
3 Mix the ground almonds with the sugar, adding just enough beaten egg to make a fairly stiff paste. Put a tablespoonful of the mixture onto the centre of each pastry circle and spread out slightly.
4 Slice the plum and apple halves neatly and arrange on top of the almond mixture. Brush the pastry with the remaining beaten egg. Sprinkle with a little caster sugar and the flaked almonds.

5 Bake for approximately 12–15 minutes, until the pastries are puffed up and golden brown. Cool for about 10 minutes, then serve warm, topped with clotted cream or single cream.

COOK'S TIP:

▓ You can bake the pastries the day before, then warm them in a low oven just before serving.

GRILLED ALMOND PEACHES WITH BLUEBERRIES

Ripe peaches or nectarines make a superb hot pudding with a few simple ingredients.

SERVES 4

Suitable for vegetarians

Peaches or nectarines, *4, halved and pitted*

Butter, *15g (½oz), softened*

Egg yolk, *1*

Golden caster sugar, *40g (1½oz)*

Ground almonds, *25g (1oz)*

Amaretti or macaroon biscuits, *25g (1oz), crushed*

Blueberries, *110g (4oz)*

Amaretto liqueur, Marsala or fruit juice, *2 tablespoons*

Greek-style natural yogurt, *to serve*

1 Preheat the grill. Put the peach or nectarine halves onto a baking sheet, cut side uppermost. Grill for 3–4 minutes.
2 Meanwhile, mix together the butter, egg yolk, half the sugar, ground almonds and crushed biscuits. Spoon into the cavities of the peaches or nectarines, then grill for a further 30–40 seconds, until lightly browned.
3 Gently heat the blueberries with the remaining sugar, 2 tablespoons of water and the liqueur, Marsala or fruit juice. Cook gently for about 2–3 minutes.
4 Lift the peaches or nectarines into four bowls, then spoon the warm blueberries on top. Serve with the Greek-style yogurt.

COOK'S TIP:

▓ Take a tiny slice from the base of each peach or nectarine half, so that they sit steadily on the baking sheet.

RHUBARB, APPLE AND STRAWBERRY FREE-FORM PIE WITH CUSTARD

A free-form pie is one where you don't have to be precise with your rolling and measuring. The fruit is simply encased in a loosely formed pastry crust for ease and speed – and the results are delicious.

SERVES 6

Suitable for vegetarians • Suitable for freezing

Plain flour, *225g (8oz)*

Salt, *pinch*

Butter, *50g (2oz), cut into pieces*

Vegetable fat, *50g (2oz), cut into pieces (for pastry-making)*

Egg, *1, beaten*

Semolina or polenta, *25g (1oz)*

Rhubarb, *225g (8oz), trimmed and chopped*

Baking apple, *1 large, peeled, cored and sliced*

Strawberries, *175g (6oz), stalks removed*

Golden caster sugar, *75g (3oz)*

Demerara sugar, *25g (1oz)*

Custard, *to serve*

1 Preheat the oven to 190°C/375°F/Gas 5. Lightly grease a baking sheet.

2 Sift the flour and salt into a bowl. Add the butter and vegetable fat and rub in with your fingertips until the mixture resembles fine breadcrumbs. Add just enough chilled water to make a smooth, but not sticky dough. Chill for 10–15 minutes.

3 Roll out the pastry to form a rough circle measuring about 35cm (14 inches) in diameter. Lift carefully onto the baking sheet. Brush the surface with beaten egg and sprinkle the semolina or polenta over the middle, to within 8cm (3 inches) of the edge. Pile the rhubarb, apple and strawberries on top and sprinkle with caster sugar. Draw up the edges of the pastry around the fruit, overlapping where necessary and pressing together.

4 Brush the pastry with beaten egg and sprinkle with demerara sugar. Bake on the middle shelf of the oven for about 25–30 minutes, until golden brown. Serve warm with custard.

COOK'S TIPS:

▓ The semolina or polenta soaks up the juices from the fruit, helping to prevent the pastry base from getting soggy.

▓ When rhubarb is out of season and strawberries are expensive, try using baking apples and blackberries instead – or plums on their own would be lovely.

cold desserts

Dairy products form the foundation of so many fabulous desserts. How could you make a Real Sherry Trifle without fresh cream? And can you imagine Rhubarb Fool, one of our classic cold English puddings, without its luscious folds of sweetened rhubarb, whipped double cream and custard?

Here you'll find some real favourites, as well as several new ideas for quick and delicious cold puddings. Select a lighter dessert when you simply want something refreshing to finish off a meal – Tangy Fruit Temptation is a good choice. Or go the whole hog with our fantastic Tiramisu – it's the kind of recipe that will have you coming back for more. Whatever your preferences, you'll be sure to find a dessert in this chapter that will tempt your tastebuds.

Getting the hang of...

CHOCOLATE PROFITEROLES

You have to get the hang of making choux pastry to make perfect profiteroles – but it's really easy when you know how. And it's worth it!

Chocolate profiteroles are probably one of our favourite desserts. Filled with whipped fresh cream and dipped into melted chocolate or drizzled with hot chocolate sauce, they are simply a taste of heaven. And the good news is that they are very easy to make, though you may have to try your hand at making choux pastry, which you might not have made before.

Choux pastry is named after the French word for cabbage – the little buns resemble small cabbages when cooked. The pastry is made with hot water, and it seems very unusual if you've never tried it before. Just make sure that you follow the recipe to the letter in order to master the art.

Chocolate éclairs are made with choux pastry too, so why not make those next time? All you do is pipe the paste into sausage shapes, allowing plenty of room in between each one for rising. Or simply make bigger buns by heaping tablespoons of the mixture onto the baking trays.

SERVES 4–6

Suitable for vegetarians

Plain flour, *65g (2½oz)*	
Salt, *small pinch*	
Water, *150ml (¼ pint)*	
Butter, *50g (2oz), cut into pieces*	
Eggs, *2, beaten*	
Double cream, *300ml (½ pint)*	
Dark chocolate, *110g (4oz), broken into pieces*	

1 Preheat the oven to 200°C/400°F/Gas 6. Lightly grease 2 baking trays. Sift the flour and salt onto a plate.

2 Put the water and butter into a medium saucepan. Heat gently so that the butter melts, then bring up to the boil. Remove from the heat, then immediately add all the flour, beating vigorously with a wooden spoon so that the mixture forms a soft ball. Return to a low heat and cook gently for about 30 seconds. Cool for about 5 minutes.

3 Gradually add the beaten eggs to the flour mixture using either a hand-held electric mixer or a wooden spoon. Make sure that you only add a little at a time, beating well between each addition, so that you end up with a mixture that is very smooth, shiny and thick.

4 Spoon the mixture into a large piping bag fitted with a star or plain piping nozzle. Pipe small mounds – about 24 in total – onto the baking sheets, allowing room for them to rise. If you prefer, you can simply put heaped teaspoonfuls on to the baking trays instead.

5 Bake for 10 minutes, then increase the oven temperature to 220°C/425°F/Gas 7. Bake for a further 10–15 minutes until the choux buns are golden brown and crisp.

6 Remove the trays from the oven and pierce each bun with a skewer, or split them with a sharp knife to let the steam escape. This prevents the buns from going soggy. Transfer to a wire rack to cool completely.

7 Whip the cream in a chilled bowl until it holds its shape. Use to fill the choux buns.

8 Melt the chocolate in a bowl placed over a saucepan of gently simmering water. Dip the choux buns in the chocolate or drizzle it over them. Leave for a few minutes or chill in the fridge to set them, then serve.

COOK'S TIPS:

▓ To enjoy profiteroles at their best, serve within a few hours of baking, filling them with cream shortly before serving, or else they will go soggy.

▓ Choux pastry rises best when the oven temperature is increased during cooking – it gives it an extra boost. Also, if you dampen the baking trays with a light sprinkling of water, the steamy atmosphere will help the buns to rise.

BRÛLÉED SUMMER FRUIT CREAMS

Desserts don't have to be complicated in order to taste fantastic – they just need a combination of fabulous flavours, put together in an imaginative way.

SERVES 6

Suitable for vegetarians

Plain biscuits, *such as digestive, 6, crushed*

Sweet sherry, red grape or orange juice, *6 tablespoons*

Raspberries, *225g (8oz)*

Strawberries, *225g (8oz), halved*

Cherries, *110g (4oz), pitted*

Redcurrants, *110g (4oz)*

Double cream, *150ml (¼ pint)*

Demerara sugar, *75g (3oz)*

Mint sprigs, *to decorate*

1   Divide the crushed biscuits between six individual heatproof dishes – cappuccino cups or teacups are ideal – and their saucers make perfect serving plates. Sprinkle the biscuits with the sherry, grape juice or orange juice.
2   Mix together the raspberries, strawberries, cherries and most of the redcurrants, reserving a sprig of redcurrants to top each dessert. Divide the fruit equally between the serving dishes.
3   Whip the cream in a chilled bowl until thick, then heap it on top of the fruit to cover it. Transfer the desserts to the refrigerator and chill for about 20 minutes, or if you are preparing the desserts in advance, chill for a few hours.
4   Preheat the grill. Stand the desserts on a baking sheet.
5   Sprinkle the demerara sugar evenly over the surface of the cream, then grill the desserts until the cream melts and the sugar starts to bubble. To achieve a good flavour the sugar and cream should start to caramelise, but keep a watchful eye on the desserts so they don't burn.
6   Cool the desserts for a few minutes, then serve, decorated with the reserved redcurrants and mint sprigs.

COOK'S TIP:

▨ When fresh summer berries are unavailable (or too expensive) simply use defrosted frozen berries instead.

TANGY FRUIT TEMPTATION

This refreshing dessert layers fresh fruit with crushed biscuits, using plain fromage frais or natural yogurt for a light taste.

SERVES 4

Suitable for vegetarians

Raspberries, *350g (12oz)*

Light muscovado sugar, *25g (1oz)*

Dessert plums, *4, pitted and sliced*

Oranges, *2 medium*

Amaretti or macaroon biscuits, *6, crushed*

Plain fromage frais or natural yogurt, *300g (11oz)*

1   Using a fork or a potato masher, crush half the raspberries in a mixing bowl. Add the sugar, stir well and leave to dissolve for a few minutes.
2   Mix the remaining raspberries with the sliced plums. Using a sharp, serrated knife, remove all the peel and pith from the oranges, then slice them into segments, removing all the membrane. Mix gently with the raspberries and plums.
3   Layer the fruit, biscuit crumbs, sweetened crushed raspberries and fromage frais or natural yogurt into 4 attractive glasses, then chill until ready to serve.

CHOCOLATE CREAM PIE WITH APRICOT SAUCE

This dessert has a lovely rich taste, which is offset beautifully by the sharper flavour of the apricot sauce.

SERVES 6–8

Suitable for freezing

Butter, *110g (4oz)*

Amaretti or digestive biscuits, *175g (6oz), crushed*

Plain chocolate, *110g (4oz), broken into pieces*

Cocoa powder, *1 tablespoon*

Amaretto liqueur or brandy, *2 tablespoons*

Cream cheese, *200g (7oz)*

Gelatine, *1 x 11g sachet*

Eggs, *2*

Dark muscovado sugar, *50g (2oz)*

Ready-to-eat dried apricots, *175g (6oz)*

Golden caster sugar, *25g (1oz)*

Double or whipping cream, *150ml (¼ pint)*

Grated chocolate, *to decorate*

1   Reserve 25g (1oz) of butter, then melt the remainder in a saucepan over a low heat. Add the biscuit crumbs, stirring to coat. Tip them into a 20cm (8 inch) loose-bottomed flan tin or dish and press into an even layer over the base. Chill in the refrigerator until firm.

2   Meanwhile, put the remaining butter, chocolate pieces, cocoa and liqueur or brandy into a large heatproof bowl. Sit the bowl over a saucepan of simmering water and allow to melt, stirring occasionally to blend. Cool slightly.

3   Beat the cream cheese in a mixing bowl to soften it, then stir it into the chocolate mixture.

4   Put 90ml (3fl oz) of just-boiled water into a bowl or jug. Sprinkle in the powdered gelatine, stirring to disperse it. Leave it to dissolve for about 3 minutes, stirring from time to time, until the liquid is perfectly clear.

5   Whilst the gelatine liquid cools slightly, put the eggs and muscovado sugar into a large heatproof bowl. Stand the bowl over the saucepan of gently simmering water and use a hand-held electric mixer to whisk them until very light and thick, and much paler in colour. Fold into the chocolate mixture, then fold in the gelatine liquid. Pour over the biscuit crumb base and chill until firm.

6   Meanwhile, make the apricot sauce. Put the apricots into a saucepan with about 150ml (¼ pint) water. Add the caster sugar and simmer until the fruit is soft, about 10 minutes. Cool, then purée in a blender until smooth.

7   Decorate the dessert with whipped fresh cream and grated chocolate, then serve with the apricot sauce.

COOK'S TIPS:

▦   Avoid adding hot gelatine liquid to cold mixtures, or else it will set on contact to form lumps – you must cool the liquid first.

▦   It's not advisable for the very young, pregnant mums or the elderly to eat raw eggs, which are included in this recipe.

THE ULTIMATE LEMON MERINGUE PIE

Enjoy a slice of this classic dessert, with its sharp-sweet filling and billowy meringue topping.

SERVES 6

Suitable for vegetarians

Sweet flan pastry:

Plain flour, *175g (6oz)*

Salt, *large pinch*

Butter, *75g (3oz), chilled and cut into pieces*

Caster sugar, *1 tablespoon*

Egg yolks, *2*

Lemon filling:

Cornflour, *25g (1oz)*

Water, *300ml (½ pint)*

Butter, *15g (½oz)*

Caster sugar, *175g (6oz)*

Lemons, *2 large, finely grated zest and juice*

Eggs, *2, separated*

1 For the pastry, mix together the flour and salt in a large bowl. Rub in the butter using your fingertips, until the mixture resembles fine breadcrumbs. Stir in the sugar, make a well in the centre and add the lightly beaten egg yolks. Stir the mixture, then draw it together to form a ball of dough.

2 Transfer the dough to a lightly floured surface and knead lightly for a few moments, then wrap and chill for 10–15 minutes.

3 Sweet flan pastry is very "short", and you may have difficulty in rolling it out, so try the following method. Put the ball of dough into the middle of a 20cm (8 inch) pie plate or ring and press out gradually using the back of a large spoon, or use your fist if you have cool hands, until you have worked the dough up the sides. Chill in the refrigerator for 15 minutes.

4 Preheat the oven to 220°C/425°F/Gas 7.

5 Prick the pastry base 6 or 7 times with a fork to let out steam. Line the base with a piece of greaseproof paper and dried beans or rice, or a piece of foil, and bake for 10 minutes. Remove the greaseproof paper and beans or foil, reduce the temperature to 190°C/375°F/Gas 5 and bake for 10 more minutes. Known as baking "blind", this ensures a crisp finish. Allow to cool.

6 For the filling, blend the cornflour with the water to make a smooth paste. Heat in a saucepan with the butter and 50g (2oz) of the sugar, stirring constantly until thickened and smooth. Remove from the heat and add the lemon zest and juice. Lightly beat the egg yolks, stir into the lemon mixture and pour into the flan case. Allow to cool.

7 Preheat the oven to 150°C/300°F/Gas 2.

8 Whisk the egg whites in a grease-free bowl until they begin to hold their shape. Gradually whisk in the remaining sugar until stiff and very glossy. Pile on top of the lemon pie, then bake in the oven for about 15–20 minutes, until the topping is golden brown. Serve warm or cold, with single cream if you like.

COOK'S TIPS:

▓ This type of meringue is soft and marshmallowy – don't expect it to be crisp.

▓ Make a speedy version by buying a prepared flan case, or use chilled or frozen sweet shortcrust pastry instead of making your own.

BERRY COMPOTE WITH HONEY OAT YOGURT

Try warmed fresh berries with cool honeyed yogurt for an easy dessert that tastes divine.

SERVES 4

Suitable for vegetarians

Strawberries, *225g (8oz), stalks removed*	**Flaked almonds,** *25g (1oz)*
Raspberries, *110g (4oz)*	**Greek-style natural yogurt,** *225g (8oz)*
Blueberries, *110g (4oz)*	**Clear honey,** *2 tablespoons*
Golden caster sugar, *40g (1½oz)*	**Mint or raspberry leaves,** *to decorate*
Porridge oats, *25g (1oz)*	

1   Put the strawberries, raspberries and blueberries into a saucepan. Add the sugar and about 6 tablespoons of cold water. Heat and simmer gently for about 2–3 minutes, until the juice begins to run from the fruit. Remove from the heat and allow to cool slightly.

2   Scatter the rolled oats and flaked almonds onto a baking sheet and toast for a couple of minutes until lightly browned. Allow to cool.

3   Mix the yogurt with the toasted oats, almonds and honey. Divide the berry compote between four serving glasses. Top with spoonfuls of the honey oat yogurt and decorate with mint or raspberry leaves.

COOK'S TIP:

▦   If you're not able to eat nuts, omit the flaked almonds.

TIRAMISU

The ultimate Italian dessert – perfect when you want to impress your guests.

SERVES 6–8

Suitable for vegetarians

Coffee granules or powder, *4 heaped teaspoons*	
Hot water, *120ml (4fl oz)*	
Marsala or Amaretto liqueur, *4 tablespoons*	
Mascarpone or cream cheese, *250g (9oz)*	
Eggs, *4, separated*	
Golden caster sugar, *65g (2½oz)*	
Double or whipping cream, *150ml (¼ pint)*	
Sponge fingers (boudoir biscuits), *about 20*	
Dark chocolate, *50g (2oz), broken into pieces*	
Cocoa powder, *2 teaspoons*	
Crystallised violets and rose petals, *to decorate (optional)*	

1 Dissolve the coffee granules or powder in the hot water. Add the Marsala or Amaretto liqueur and leave until completely cold.

2 Spoon the mascarpone or cream cheese into a very large bowl and beat it with a wooden spoon to soften it.

3 In a separate bowl, whisk the egg yolks and caster sugar together until pale, very light and fluffy. Use a hand-held electric mixer for this – it will take about 4–5 minutes. Fold into the cheese with a large metal spoon.

4 In a large grease-free bowl and with scrupulously clean beaters, whisk the egg whites until they hold their shape. Fold them into the cheese mixture. Use the same bowl for whipping the cream until it holds its shape, then fold this into the cheese mixture too.

5 One by one, dip half the sponge fingers into the coffee mixture, placing them as you go into the base of a large serving dish. Spread half the cheese mixture over the top.

6 Dip the remaining sponge fingers into the coffee mixture and arrange them in the dish in an even layer. Spoon the remaining cheese mixture over the top and level the surface. Cover with cling film and chill for 3–4 hours, or overnight if preferred.

7 Melt the chocolate in a heatproof basin placed over a saucepan of gently simmering water, taking care that no water gets into the chocolate. Tip the melted chocolate onto a marble slab or chopping board, and refrigerate until firm. To make curls, push a sharp knife across the surface of the chocolate. Keep them cool.

8 When ready to serve, sprinkle the surface of the tiramisu with the cocoa powder, then with the chocolate curls. Finish with a few crystallised violets and rose petals, if you like.

COOK'S TIPS:

▧ As raw eggs are used, make sure they are very fresh and from a reliable source. It's not advisable for the very young, pregnant mums or the very old to eat raw eggs. If you can't eat them, fold a total of 300ml (½ pint) of whipped double or whipping cream into the cheese mixture, adding the sugar to the cheese first.

▧ Dip the sponge fingers briefly into the coffee mixture – or else they will disintegrate before you can assemble them in the dish.

▧ Use brandy or rum instead of Marsala or Amaretto, if you prefer.

SUMMER FRUIT PAVLOVA

Make a spectacular finish to a special meal with this stunning dessert.

SERVES 6–8

Suitable for vegetarians

Egg whites, *4 (from large eggs)*	
Golden caster sugar, *225g (8oz)*	
Double or whipping cream, *300ml (½ pint)*	
Strawberries, *110g (4oz), halved*	
Kiwi fruit, *1, peeled and sliced*	
Nectarine or peach, *1, sliced*	
Red or green grapes, *75g (3oz)*	
Ground cinnamon, *¼ teaspoon*	

1   Preheat the oven to 140°C/275°F/Gas 1. Line a baking sheet with non-stick baking parchment and draw a 25cm (10 inch) circle on it, using a plate or cake tin to guide you.

2   In a large grease-free bowl and using a hand-held electric whisk, whip the egg whites until they hold their shape. Gradually add the sugar, whisking well between each addition, until the egg whites are very stiff and glossy.

3   Spread the meringue in an even layer over the marked out circle, then transfer to the middle shelf of the oven and bake for 2–3 hours. The meringue is "dried out" rather than cooked at this low temperature. If you have an Aga or Rayburn, leave it in the slow oven for several hours to dry out. Remove from the oven, cool completely, then carefully peel away from the parchment.

4   Whip the cream until thick, then pile onto the meringue base. Decorate with the strawberries, kiwi fruit, nectarine or peach and grapes, then serve, sprinkled with a little ground cinnamon.

COOK'S TIPS:

▦ Try to make the meringue base at least one day before you need it, then store it in an airtight tin or wrap well.

▦ If you like, carefully slice the meringue base into portions before you top it with cream and fruit. This way you can serve it without it (or you!) falling apart.

APPLE AND LEMON SNOW

Cool down with this refreshing dessert made with puréed apples, whipped egg white, fromage frais and lemon – frozen until semi-solid.

SERVES 4

Suitable for vegetarians
Suitable for freezing

Cooking apples, *450g (1lb), peeled, cored and chopped*

Fromage frais or Greek-style natural yogurt, *110g (4oz)*

Lemon zest, *1 teaspoon, finely grated*

Lemon juice, *2 tablespoons*

Egg whites, *2*

Caster sugar, *50g (2oz)*

Lemon zest, apple slices and mint leaves, *to decorate*

1   Cook the apples in a small amount of water until soft and pulpy – this will take about 8–10 minutes. Mash or purée them, then leave them to cool.
2   Add the fromage frais or yogurt, lemon zest and lemon juice to the cooled apples, stirring well to mix.
3   In a grease-free bowl, whisk the egg whites until they hold their shape, then whisk in the sugar gradually until they form stiff peaks. Add to the apple mixture and fold through, using a large metal spoon, then chill in the freezer until semi-solid – about 1–1½ hours.
4   Divide between 4 serving glasses, then serve at once, decorated with lemon zest, apple slices and mint leaves.

COOK'S TIPS:

▓ You can freeze these desserts until solid – though remember to remove them from the freezer about 20 minutes before eating.

▓ Please remember that it's not advisable for the very young, pregnant mums or the very old to eat raw eggs, which this recipe contains.

LEMON AND GREEK YOGURT POTS

Bake these lemony custard cheesecakes in individual dishes so that you can serve them easily.

SERVES 6

Suitable for vegetarians

Low-fat soft cheese or cream cheese, *400g (14oz)*

Lemon zest, *2 teaspoons, finely grated*

Golden caster sugar, *75g (3oz)*

Greek-style natural yogurt, *300g (11oz)*

Vanilla extract, *1 teaspoon*

Eggs, *3*

Raspberries or redcurrants, *to decorate*

Mint leaves, *to decorate*

Icing sugar, *for sprinkling*

1 Preheat the oven to 180°C/350°F/Gas 4.

2 Beat the cheese with a wooden spoon until softened, then beat in the lemon zest, sugar, yogurt and vanilla extract.

3 Beat the eggs, add to the cheese mixture and mix thoroughly. Pour into 6 individual flan dishes or ramekin dishes. Stand the dishes in a large roasting pan and pour in enough warm water to come halfway up their sides. Bake for 30–35 minutes, until set.

4 Serve barely warm or chilled, topped with raspberries or redcurrants, and decorated with mint leaves and sprinkled with icing sugar.

COOK'S TIP:

▧ Try to buy unwaxed lemons for this recipe – or give ordinary ones a thorough scrub before grating the zest.

REAL SHERRY TRIFLE

SERVES 6–8

Suitable for vegetarians

Milk, *600ml (1 pint)*

Vanilla extract, *1½ teaspoons*

Egg yolks, *2*

Eggs, *2*

Cornflour, *1 tablespoon*

Golden caster sugar, *40g (1½oz)*

Jam Swiss rolls, *2, sliced*

Sherry (medium sweet), *150ml (¼ pint)*

Orange juice, *150ml (¼ pint)*

Banana, *1 large, sliced*

Strawberries, *110g (4oz), sliced*

Seedless grapes (red or green), *175g (6oz), halved*

Kiwi fruit, *2, peeled and sliced*

Double cream, *300ml (½ pint)*

Redcurrants or raspberries, *to decorate*

Grated chocolate or cocoa powder, *for sprinkling*

1 Put the milk and vanilla extract into a heavy-based saucepan and heat until lukewarm. Beat the egg yolks and eggs together in a large heatproof bowl and blend in the cornflour. Add the warm milk and stir well. Sit the bowl over a large saucepan of simmering water. Stir with a wooden spoon until the custard thickens – it will take about 15–20 minutes.

2 Pour the thickened custard into a bowl and sprinkle the surface with the sugar, without stirring it in. This will help to prevent a skin from forming as the custard cools. Allow to cool completely.

3 Arrange the slices of Swiss roll in the base of a trifle dish. Sprinkle with the sherry. Mix together the orange juice, banana, strawberries, grapes and kiwi fruit and spoon into the trifle dish. Allow a few minutes to soak in, then stir the cooled custard and pour it over the fruits. Cover and refrigerate for at least 1 hour.

4 Whip the cream in a chilled bowl until it holds its shape. Spoon about one-third of it into a piping bag fitted with a star nozzle. Spread the rest over the surface of the trifle, then pipe rosettes around the edge. Decorate with redcurrants or raspberries, then cover and chill until ready to serve, sprinkled with a little grated chocolate or cocoa powder.

COOK'S TIPS:

■ Chill a large mixing bowl thoroughly before using it for whipping cream – it will keep the cream cold, helping you to whip it more quickly. Make sure that the cream itself is well-chilled too. Use a balloon or spiral whisk in preference to electric beaters – you have more control, and there is less chance of over-whipping it.

■ Don't worry if you are hopeless at piping cream – just use a teaspoon to spoon it around the edge of the trifle instead. It will look just as attractive when decorated.

■ Save time by using fresh chilled custard instead of making your own.

RHUBARB AND GINGER FOOL

This simple dessert is absolute heaven to eat – and makes the most of a rather underrated fruit.

SERVES 6

Suitable for vegetarians

Rhubarb, *675g (1½lb), trimmed and chopped*

Golden caster sugar, *110g (4oz)*

Double or whipping cream, *300ml (½ pint)*

Cold, thick custard, *150ml (¼ pint)*

Stem ginger in syrup, *25g (1oz), very finely sliced or chopped*

1 Put the rhubarb into a saucepan with the sugar and about 3 tablespoons of water. Cover and simmer over a very low heat for about 10 minutes, so that the rhubarb cooks down gently until soft and pulpy.

2 Allow the rhubarb to cool completely, then crush it lightly with a fork. Spoon a little into the base of 6 serving glasses.

3 Whip the cream in a chilled bowl until it holds its shape, then fold in the cold custard and rhubarb and most of the ginger. You don't have to mix it thoroughly – the dessert looks and tastes nice if it is just swirled together. Divide between the glasses and chill until ready to serve. Decorate with the reserved ginger.

GAELIC COFFEE CREAMS

Try this wonderful recipe – inspired by the delicious flavour of a Gaelic coffee. A wonderful way to round off a special meal.

SERVES 4

Suitable for vegetarians

Eggs, *2*

Dark muscovado sugar, *50g (2oz) + extra, for sprinkling*

Whisky or brandy, *3 tablespoons*

Coffee granules or powder, *1 tablespoon*

Double or whipping cream, *200ml (7fl oz)*

1 Put the eggs and sugar into a large heatproof bowl. Add the whisky or brandy and coffee. Stir until the coffee granules or powder have dissolved.

2 Sit the bowl over a saucepan of gently simmering water and whisk with a hand-held electric mixer until very thick, pale and fluffy. This will take about 4–5 minutes. Remove from the heat and allow to cool.

3 In a separate bowl, whip the cream until it holds its shape. Reserve about one third of the cream and fold the remainder through the cooled coffee mixture, using a large metal spoon. Divide between four serving glasses.

4 Top each dessert with the reserved cream and sprinkle each one with about ½ teaspoon of dark muscovado sugar. Serve at once.

COOK'S TIP:

▪ Use Tia Maria liqueur or dark rum as an alternative to the whisky or brandy.

KEY LIME PIES

Try this easy variation of lemon meringue – made with limes and condensed milk.

SERVES 4

Suitable for vegetarians

Butter, *50g (2oz)*	
Digestive biscuits, *110g (4oz), crushed*	
Eggs, *2, separated*	
Condensed milk, *1 x 405g can*	
Limes, *2, finely grated zest and juice*	
Green food colouring, *3–4 drops*	
Caster sugar, *50g (2oz)*	

1   Melt the butter in a saucepan and add the biscuit crumbs, stirring to coat. Spoon them into four individual baking dishes or flan dishes, pressing them over the base. Chill in the refrigerator for about 15 minutes.

2   Preheat the oven to 180°C/350°F/Gas 4.

3   Beat the egg yolks and condensed milk together, then stir in the lime zest and juice. Add a few drops of food colouring to give a pale green colour. Pour into the prepared dishes and bake for 15–20 minutes, until set.

4   In a grease-free bowl and using perfectly clean beaters, whisk the egg whites until they hold their shape. Add the sugar gradually, whisking well to give stiff, glossy peaks. Pipe or pile the meringue topping onto the lime pies. Return to the oven and bake for about 5–6 minutes, until the tops are golden brown. Serve warm or cold.

COOK'S TIP:

▦ The green colouring isn't essential, so leave it out if you don't have any.

BAKED VANILLA CHEESECAKE

Baked cheesecakes taste delicious – and they don't have to be difficult or too expensive to make. Try this recipe to prove the point.

SERVES 6–8

Suitable for vegetarians

Butter, *3oz (75g)*

Oatmeal or digestive biscuits, *150g (5oz), crushed*

Cream cheese or low-fat soft cheese, *350g (12oz)*

Greek-style natural yogurt, *150g (5oz)*

Golden caster sugar, *110g (4oz)*

Lemon zest, *1 teaspoon, finely grated*

Vanilla extract, *2 teaspoons*

Eggs, *3, separated*

Icing sugar, *for sprinkling (optional)*

1   Preheat the oven to 170°C/325°F/Gas 3. Grease a 20cm (8 inch) loose-based cake tin and line with greaseproof paper.

2   Melt the butter in a large saucepan, remove from the heat and add the biscuit crumbs, stirring well to coat them. Tip them into the prepared tin, spread out and press over the base. Chill for about 10 minutes.

3   Meanwhile, beat the cream cheese or soft cheese in a large bowl with a wooden spoon to soften it. Add the yogurt, sugar, lemon zest, vanilla extract and egg yolks and beat until combined.

4   In a large grease-free bowl, whisk the egg whites until stiff. Fold them gently into the cream cheese mixture, using a large metal spoon. Pour over the biscuit crumb base.

5   Bake in the oven for approximately 1 hour, until set and firm. If necessary, cook for a few minutes longer. Remove from the oven and stand the tin on a cooling rack – the cheesecake will deflate, but don't worry as this is meant to happen. Cool in the tin.

6   Remove the cheesecake from the tin and peel away the lining paper. Serve, sprinkled with icing sugar, or top with fresh or poached fruit.

COOK'S TIPS:

▧ For a raisin cheesecake add 50g (2oz) of seedless raisins to the mixture with the egg yolks.

▧ For a chocolate cheesecake, use plain chocolate digestive biscuits for the base, then swirl 110g (4oz) of cooled melted chocolate into the mixture before adding the egg whites.

home baking

Flick through the pages of this chapter and before you know it, you'll be getting out the ingredients for indulging in a bit of home baking. And why not? Baking can be really rewarding – the sight and smell of a cake in the oven is very satisfying – and the taste as you and your friends and family tuck in is even better.

This home baking chapter contains some classic favourites. If you're new to baking, you'll really get the hang of making a batch of scones with our easy-to-follow recipe for guaranteed results. Or enjoy the zing of citrus flavoured Soaked Lime and Lemon Sponge. If you prefer savoury bakes, try your hand at making Rosemary, Onion and Cheddar Focaccia or simple-to-make Soda Bread – perfect served with a hunk of cheese. Enjoy!

Getting the hang of...

SCONES

Simple to make – once you have the know-how – scones are utterly delicious to eat, especially when served West Country style, with lashings of clotted cream and strawberry jam.

Home made scones are so much better than shop bought ones, and they are very quick and easy to make – you can bake a batch within half an hour. The best way to serve them is when they are still warm from the oven, spread with butter, or topped with jam and cream. Follow our tips for making fruit or cheese scones too – once you get the hang of the recipe, you'll want to make them again and again.

Try not to overhandle the dough, and use a light touch when rolling it out. Make sure that you don't roll out the dough too thinly either – you're making scones, not biscuits, so it needs to be at least 2.5cm (1 inch) thick.

MAKES 12

Suitable for vegetarians
Suitable for freezing

Self-raising flour, *450g (1lb)*

Salt, *generous pinch*

Butter, *110g (4oz), chilled and diced*

Golden caster sugar *50g (2oz)*

Milk, *300ml (½ pint) + extra, to glaze*

Butter, clotted cream and strawberry jam, *to serve*

1   Preheat the oven to 220°C/425°F/Gas 7. Lightly grease a baking sheet.

2   Sift the flour and salt into a large mixing bowl and add the butter. Using your fingertips, rub the butter into the flour, lifting your hands as you do so to encourage more air into the mixture, until it looks like fine breadcrumbs.

3   Stir the sugar into the mixture, then gradually add just enough milk to make a soft, but not sticky dough, drawing the mixture together with a round-bladed knife or palette knife. Try to avoid using your hands, as this warms the mixture.

4   Turn the dough out onto a lightly floured surface, flour your hands a little, then knead the dough lightly for a few moments. Wrap and chill for 10–15 minutes.

5   Using a lightly floured rolling pin, roll out the dough to about 2.5cm (1 inch) thick, then use a 5cm (2 inch) plain or fluted cutter to stamp out rounds. Don't twist the cutter when you are doing this, just press it straight through the dough. This will help your scones to rise evenly. Gather any trimmings together, re-roll and cut out more scones.

6   Arrange the scones on the baking sheet. Brush the surface with a little milk and transfer to the oven. Bake for 12–15 minutes towards the top of the oven, until well-risen and golden brown. Cool for a few moments, then transfer to a cooling rack. Serve warm, with butter, clotted cream and jam.

COOK'S TIPS:

▓   For fruit scones add 50g (2oz) of sultanas, raisins or dried cherries, stirring them in before adding the milk. For date and walnut scones, add 50g (2oz) of chopped dates and 25g (1oz) of chopped walnuts.

▓   To make cheese scones, omit the sugar and add 75g (3oz) of grated mature Cheddar cheese to the mixture before adding the milk. Sprinkle a little extra cheese on top of the scones before baking.

SOAKED LIME AND LEMON SPONGE

A buttery cake that's soaked with a hot citrus syrup to give it a really delicious, moist flavour.

SERVES 8–10

Suitable for vegetarians
Suitable for freezing

Butter, *110g (4oz)*

Golden caster sugar, *110g (4oz)*

Eggs, *3, beaten*

Lemon, *1 large, finely grated zest and juice*

Lime, *1, finely grated zest and juice*

Self-raising flour, *225g (8oz)*

Salt, *pinch*

Icing sugar, *50g (2oz)*

1 Preheat the oven to 180°C/350°F/Gas 4. Grease and line a 900g (2lb) loaf tin.

2 Cream the butter and caster sugar together until light and fluffy. Gradually add the eggs, beating well between each addition. Stir in half the lemon and lime zest.

3 Sift the flour and salt together and add to the creamed mixture, folding in gently with a large metal spoon. Transfer the mixture to the prepared tin and level the surface.

4 Bake for approximately 1 hour until the cake is cooked. Test with a fine skewer – it should come out clean. Stand the cake tin on a cooling rack and pierce the hot cake about 10 times with a skewer, right through to its base.

5 Heat the lemon juice, lime juice and remaining zest with the icing sugar until the sugar dissolves. Slowly pour over the cake whilst hot. Allow the cake to cool and absorb the citrus syrup before you remove it from the tin.

COOK'S TIP:

■ If you don't want to use a lime, use two medium lemons instead.

RICH FRUIT CAKE

The secret of this cake's moist, mature flavour lies in soaking the fruit in brandy or rum for several days before you bake the cake – so plan ahead. The cake is perfect for a special occasion – Christmas, a wedding or anniversary.

MAKES 1 x 20cm (8 inch) ROUND CAKE

Suitable for vegetarians

Seedless raisins, *450g (1lb)*

Sultanas, *450g (1lb)*

Currants, *225g (8oz)*

Glacé cherries, *110g (4oz), halved*

Brandy or dark rum, *150ml (5fl oz) + 4–5 tablespoons*

Butter, *175g (6oz), at room temperature*

Dark muscovado sugar, *175g (6oz)*

Eggs, *4, beaten*

Ground almonds, *110g (4oz)*

Flaked almonds, *50g (2oz)*

Orange, *1 small, finely grated zest and juice*

Plain flour, *300g (11oz)*

Salt, *¼ teaspoon*

Ground mixed spice, *1 heaped teaspoon*

1 About 4–5 days before you plan to bake the cake, put the raisins, sultanas, currants and cherries into a large bowl and cover with just-boiled water. Soak for 10 minutes, stirring occasionally, then drain really well. Add the brandy or rum, stir well, then cover and keep in a cool place for 4–5 days, stirring every day.

2 When ready to make the cake, grease a deep 20cm (8 inch) round cake tin with a little vegetable oil or butter, then line it with double thickness greaseproof paper. Lightly grease the paper with butter.

3 Preheat the oven to 150°C/300°F/Gas 2.

4 In a very large bowl, beat together the butter and sugar until light and fluffy. Add the eggs a little at a time, beating well between each addition. Stir in the ground almonds, flaked almonds, orange zest and juice. The mixture may curdle, but don't worry.

5 Sift together the flour, salt and spice, then add to the creamed mixture and fold in, using a large metal spoon.

6 Tip the soaked dried fruit, including any liquid, into the cake mixture and fold in, mixing thoroughly. Turn into the prepared cake tin and level the surface.

7 Bake for approximately 2½–3 hours. Check after 2 hours, covering the surface with double-thickness brown paper if the top is dark enough. To test that the cake is cooked, pierce the surface with a fine skewer – if it comes out clean, the cake is cooked.

8 Stand the tin on a wire rack and allow to cool completely. To store, wrap the cake in greaseproof paper and place in an airtight tin.

9 A few days after baking the cake, pierce the surface several times with a fine skewer, then slowly pour 4 or 5 tablespoons of brandy or rum over the surface, so that it soaks in. Wrap and store as before.

COOK'S TIP:

▓ Do remember that all ovens vary – so your cake may take slightly less or more time than someone else's.

CLASSIC VICTORIA SPONGE

When you have a slice of this fabulous home-made cake, you'll vow never to buy shop-bought cakes again.

**MAKES ONE 18cm (7 inch) CAKE –
APPROXIMATELY 8 SLICES**

Suitable for vegetarians • Suitable for freezing

Vegetable oil or butter, *for greasing*

Butter, *110g (4oz), cut into pieces*

Golden caster sugar, *110g (4oz), plus extra, for sprinkling*

Eggs, *2, beaten*

Vanilla extract, *½ teaspoon*

Self-raising flour, *110g (4oz)*

Salt, *small pinch*

Milk, *1 tablespoon*

Strawberry jam, *3–4 tablespoons*

Double or whipping cream, *120ml (4fl oz)*

1 Position the oven shelves towards the centre of the oven. Preheat the oven to 180°C/350°F/ Gas 4. Lightly grease two 18cm (7 inch) sandwich tins with vegetable oil or butter, line their bases with circles of greaseproof paper, then lightly grease the paper.

2 Beat together the butter and caster sugar in a large mixing bowl with a wooden spoon or hand-held electric mixer until the mixture is very pale in colour and light and fluffy in texture.

3 Gradually add the eggs to the creamed mixture, beating well between each addition. If the mixture looks like it is about to curdle, add 1 teaspoon of the flour when you add the beaten egg. Stir in the vanilla extract.

4 Sift the flour and salt into the bowl, then use a large metal spoon to fold it in. Do this as lightly as possible – the trick is to avoid losing the air you have so carefully beaten in. The mixture should have a soft, dropping consistency. To check, pick up a large spoonful and suspend it over the bowl – it should drop off quite easily. If it doesn't, lightly stir in the milk.

5 Divide the mixture equally between the prepared tins and level the surfaces. Transfer to the oven and bake for 18–20 minutes. To test that the cakes are cooked, the surfaces should be golden brown, and when touched lightly with your finger they should spring back into place. If they are cooked, put the tins on to a wire rack to cool for a few minutes.

6 Remove the cakes from their tins and cool on a wire rack, then remove the lining paper.

7 When completely cool, sandwich the cakes together with strawberry jam and whipped cream, then sprinkle the top with caster sugar.

COOK'S TIPS:

▓ Always use the correct cake tin specified in a recipe – it's very important. To make a 20cm (8 inch) cake, use 175g (6oz) butter, 175g (6oz) caster sugar and 175g (6oz) self-raising flour, and 3 eggs.

▓ Improvise if you don't possess a wire cooling rack – use the rack from the grill pan.

▓ For a special occasion, slice a few strawberries to add to the filling, then decorate the top with strawberries and redcurrants or raspberries.

APPLE AND APRICOT CRUMBLE CAKE

This recipe doubles as a dessert or a cake. Either way, there will hardly be a crumb left. Try it another time with just a layer of apples.

SERVES 8–10

Suitable for vegetarians • Suitable for freezing

Light muscovado sugar, *175g (6oz)*

Crunchy tropical fruits oat cereal or coarse porridge oats, *225g (8oz)*

Wholemeal self-raising flour, *225g (8oz)*

Mixed spice, *1 teaspoon*

Butter, *225g (8oz), melted*

Cox's apples, *2, peeled, cored and sliced*

Ready-to-eat dried apricots, *175g (6oz) roughly chopped*

Sultanas, *25g (1oz)*

Demerara sugar, *2 tablespoons*

Dairy ice cream, custard or Greek-style natural yogurt, *to serve*

1   Preheat the oven to 180°C/350°F/Gas 4. Grease and line a 18cm (7 inch) round loose-based cake tin.
2   Mix together the sugar, cereal or porridge oats, flour and spice.
3   Stir the melted butter into the dry ingredients, then tip half the mixture into the prepared cake tin. Press down lightly and arrange half the apples, apricots and sultanas on top. Sprinkle with the remaining crumble mixture, then the remaining fruit. Press down lightly and sprinkle with the demerara sugar.
4   Bake for 35–40 minutes until firm and golden brown. Stand the tin on a wire rack and allow to cool for 15–20 minutes, then remove from the tin. Carefully remove the lining paper.
5   Serve the cake warm or cold with dairy ice cream, custard or Greek-style natural yogurt.

COOK'S TIP:

▨   Buy vanilla flavoured ready-to-eat dried apricots if you can find them – they taste delicious in this recipe.

GROUND ALMOND CAKE

An easy plain cake that has a lovely flavour and deliciously nutty texture. Enjoy a slice with a cup of tea or coffee.

SERVES 12–16

Suitable for vegetarians • Suitable for freezing

Butter, *110g (4oz)*

Golden caster sugar, *110g (4oz)*

Eggs, *3, beaten*

Vanilla extract, *1 teaspoon*

Ground almonds, *110g (4oz)*

Self-raising flour, *110g (4oz)*

Semolina, *25g (1oz)*

Salt, *pinch*

Almonds, *25g (1oz), roughly chopped*

Sugar cubes, *10, lightly crushed (optional)*

1   Preheat the oven to 170°C/325°F/Gas 3. Grease and line an 18cm (7 inch) square or 20cm (8 inch) round cake tin.
2   Cream together the butter and sugar until light and fluffy. Beat in the eggs and vanilla extract.
3   Fold in the ground almonds, flour, semolina and salt, using a large metal spoon.
4   Tip the mixture into the prepared cake tin and level the surface. Sprinkle with the chopped almonds and crushed sugar cubes, if using.
5   Transfer to the oven and bake for 35–40 minutes until risen and golden brown, and the surface is springy, yet firm to the touch. Cool on a wire rack for 15 minutes, then lift the cake from the tin and cool completely, or serve when warm.

BANANA CAKE

A good banana cake is difficult to beat – and this is a very good banana cake!

SERVES 8

Suitable for vegetarians • Suitable for freezing (without frosting)

Self-raising flour, *225g (8oz)*

Salt, *pinch*

Butter, *110g (4oz), chilled and cut into pieces*

Light muscovado sugar, *110g (4oz)*

Eggs, *2, beaten*

Vanilla extract, *1 teaspoon*

Ripe bananas, *450g (1lb) (weighed with skins)*

Walnuts, *25g (1oz), chopped*

Milk, *1–2 tablespoons*

Frosting:

Cream cheese, *350g (12oz)*

Lemon zest, *1 teaspoon, grated, plus a few shreds, to decorate*

Icing sugar, *1 tablespoon*

Dried banana chips, *15g (½oz), optional*

Mixed nuts, *25g (1oz), chopped, optional*

1 Preheat the oven to 180°C/350°F/Gas 4. Check the oven shelves – the cake needs to be baked in the centre of the oven. Grease and line a 20cm (8 inch) cake tin.

2 Sift the flour and salt into a large mixing bowl. Add the chilled butter and, using your fingertips, rub into the flour until the mixture resembles fine breadcrumbs. Stir in the sugar.

3 Beat the eggs and vanilla extract together. Peel the bananas and mash them using a potato masher or a fork.

4 Add the eggs, mashed bananas and walnuts to the cake mixture. Stir everything together until combined. Check the texture – the mixture should have a soft, dropping consistency, which means that when you lift up a generous spoonful from the bowl, it will drop off in a moment or two. If the mixture is too stiff, stir in 1–2 tablespoons of milk.

5 Turn the mixture into the prepared tin and level the surface. Bake for 55 minutes–1 hour. Remember that ovens vary – your cake may need a little longer. To test that it is cooked, insert a fine skewer into the centre of the cake. If it comes out clean, the cake is cooked. If not, bake for a little longer.

6 Stand the cooked cake on a wire rack and allow to cool completely in the tin. When cool, remove the lining paper and split in half horizontally.

7 Mix together the cream cheese, grated lemon zest and icing sugar. Spread half over one cut surface of the cake, then sandwich the two halves together. Spread the remaining frosting over the top and decorate with banana chips, chopped nuts and lemon zest.

COOK'S TIPS:

▨ Keep the finished cake covered and refrigerated – let it come up to room temperature before you eat it.

▨ Buy dried banana chips from health food stores and major supermarkets, or use chopped ready-to-eat apricots instead.

SHORTBREAD

A wonderful recipe for shortbread – buttery, rich, crumbly and melt-in-the-mouth. Utterly delicious!

MAKES ABOUT 16 BISCUITS

Suitable for vegetarians • Suitable for freezing

Vegetable oil, *for greasing*

Butter, *225g (8oz), at room temperature, cut into pieces*

Golden caster sugar, *110g (4oz)*

Plain flour, *350g (12oz)*

Salt, *pinch*

1 Preheat the oven to 180°C/350°F/Gas 4. Lightly grease two baking sheets with a little vegetable oil.

2 Put the butter into a large mixing bowl with the caster sugar. Beat with a wooden spoon until thoroughly incorporated – although it isn't necessary to beat until light and fluffy.

3 Sift in the flour and salt and work into the mixture with the wooden spoon, until it looks like crumbs.

4 Gather the mixture together with your hands and form into a ball. Transfer to a lightly floured surface and knead lightly and quickly until smooth, but avoid too much handling.

5 Using a lightly floured rolling pin, roll out the dough to a thickness of about 1cm (½ inch). Cut out triangles – you don't have to be too precise – or stamp out circles, using a 5cm (2 inch) biscuit cutter. Carefully lift onto the baking sheets.

6 Bake in the oven for about 15 minutes until light golden brown. Cool for a few minutes, transfer to a wire rack to cool completely, then store in an airtight tin.

COOK'S TIPS:

▓ Try adding about 40g (1½oz) of stem ginger in syrup, rinsed and patted dry. Chop it finely, then stir it into the mixture before you draw it together.

▓ Just before baking, sprinkle the biscuits with a few flaked almonds and a little demerara sugar.

NATURAL YOGURT ORANGE CAKE

This all-in-one cake couldn't be easier to make. You just beat all the ingredients together for one minute – then bake for an hour.

SERVES 8–10

Suitable for vegetarians • Suitable for freezing

Butter, *150g (5oz), melted and cooled slightly*

Orange, *1 large, finely grated zest and juice*

Golden caster sugar, *150g (5oz)*

Natural yogurt, *150g (5oz)*

Vanilla extract, *1 teaspoon*

Self-raising flour, *250g (9oz)*

Salt, *pinch*

Eggs, *2 large*

Orange slices, *3, halved*

1   Preheat the oven to 170°C/325°F/Gas 3. Grease a 20cm (8 inch) round cake tin with a little melted butter and then line it with greaseproof paper.

2   Put the orange juice into a jug and add one tablespoon of the caster sugar. Set aside.

3   Put the orange zest into a large mixing bowl and add the remaining sugar, melted butter, yogurt, vanilla extract, flour, salt and eggs. Beat vigorously for 1 minute with a wooden spoon.

4   Pour the mixture into the prepared tin and top with the orange slices. Transfer to the middle shelf of the oven and bake for approximately 1 hour, or until risen and springy when lightly touched.

5   Stand the cake tin on a cooling rack, and whilst hot, slowly spoon the orange juice mixture over the cake. Allow to cool in the tin.

COOK'S TIPS:

▌ Try using lemon zest and juice for a change.

▌ Cut into slices, wrap in freezer wrap, and freeze for up to 2 months – then you can take out the number of slices you need.

YORKSHIRE CURD TART

Fresh dairy ingredients are the makings of this traditional Yorkshire cheesecake.

SERVES 6

Suitable for vegetarians • Suitable for freezing

Plain flour, *175g (6oz)*

Salt, *pinch*

Butter, *40g (1½ oz), chilled and cut into pieces*

White vegetable fat, *40g (1½ oz), chilled and cut into pieces*

Caster sugar, *25g (1oz) + 2 teaspoons*

Eggs, *2, beaten*

Single cream, *4 tablespoons*

Natural cottage cheese, *225g (8oz)*

Vanilla extract, *½ teaspoon*

Currants, *50g (2oz)*

Lemon zest, *½ teaspoon*

Ground nutmeg, *pinch (freshly ground, if possible)*

Fresh double or single cream, *to serve*

1 Sift the flour and salt into a large mixing bowl. Add the butter and vegetable fat, and rub in using your fingertips until the mixture resembles fine breadcrumbs. Stir in 2 teaspoons of caster sugar, then enough chilled water to make a firm dough. Knead lightly for a few moments then wrap and refrigerate for about 10 minutes.

2 Preheat the oven to 200°C/400°F/Gas 6.

3 Turn the pastry out onto a lightly floured surface, roll out and use to line a 23cm (9 inch) pie plate or flan dish. Use any trimmings to decorate the edge. Prick the base, line with foil and bake blind for 10 minutes. Remove the foil and allow to cool slightly.

4 Reduce the oven temperature to 180°C/350°F/Gas 4.

5 To make the filling, beat the eggs and single cream together in a bowl. Add the cottage cheese, remaining sugar, vanilla extract, currants and lemon zest. Pour into the pastry case and sprinkle with ground nutmeg.

6 Bake in the oven for approximately 35 minutes, until the filling has set and turned a light golden brown. Serve warm with fresh double or single cream.

COOK'S TIP:

▪ When time is short, use a bought pre-baked sweet shortcrust pastry case.

BUTTER GARLAND BISCUITS

These attractive biscuits taste as good as they look. At Christmas, they look wonderful wrapped and tied to the tree with ribbon.

MAKES ABOUT 16

Suitable for vegetarians • Suitable for freezing

Butter, *225g (8oz)*	
Golden caster sugar, *75g (3oz)*	
Vanilla extract, *1 teaspoon*	
Plain flour, *250g (9oz)*	
Milk, *2–3 tablespoons*	
Glacé cherries and angelica, *to decorate*	

1   Preheat the oven to 180°C/350°F/Gas 4. Line two baking sheets with non-stick baking parchment.
2   Cream the butter and sugar together until light and fluffy, using a hand-held electric whisk, if you wish. Beat in the vanilla extract, then sift in the flour and work it into the mixture. Add just enough milk to give a smooth, stiff piping consistency.
3   Fit a star nozzle into a large piping bag, then spoon in the biscuit mixture. Pipe the mixture into 5cm (2 inch) circles on the baking sheets, allowing some room for them to spread. Decorate with glacé cherries and angelica.
4   Bake for 15–20 minutes until pale golden brown. Cool for a few minutes, then transfer to a wire rack to cool completely.

COOK'S TIP:

▇   For a different decoration, forget the cherries and angelica and drizzle the cooled biscuits with melted chocolate instead.

FRESH LEMON CURD

This wonderful recipe for lemon curd has sneaked into the baking chapter because it tastes so good with fresh scones, as a filling for Victoria Sponge or a topping for cheesecake. If you've never made it before, you must have a go – it only takes about 30 minutes from start to finish. It has a fantastic flavour that really can't be matched by anything you can buy.

MAKES 2 x 350g (12oz) POTS

Suitable for vegetarians

Unsalted butter, *225g (8oz)*	
Eggs, *4*	
Golden caster sugar, *225g (8oz)*	
Lemons, *2 large, unwaxed or thoroughly scrubbed*	

1   Melt the butter over a low heat, being careful to make sure that it doesn't get too hot.
2   In a large heatproof bowl, whisk together the eggs and sugar. Finely grate the zest from the lemons and squeeze the juice. Add to the bowl and whisk together, then stir in the melted butter.
3   Set the bowl over a large saucepan of gently simmering water and stir with a wooden spoon until the mixture is thick enough to leave a soft trail on the surface when lifted. This takes about 20 minutes. (The mixture will thicken more as it cools.)
4   Pour into sterilised jars and cover. Cool, then refrigerate and use within two weeks.

COOK'S TIPS:

▇   When grating the zest from lemons, be sure to remove only the yellow part, as any white pith will add bitterness.

▇   Try the lemon curd spooned on to fresh plain scones, topped with crème fraîche, thick Greek-style yogurt or clotted cream.

SODA BREAD

Soda bread is simple and quick to make and uses bicarbonate of soda instead of yeast to make it rise. It won't keep as long as conventional bread, so eat it when fresh, or toast it lightly the day after baking.

MAKES 1 LOAF (10–12 SLICES)

Suitable for vegetarians • Suitable for freezing

Wholemeal plain flour, *225g (8oz)*

Strong white bread flour, *225g (8oz)*

Salt, *1½ teaspoons*

Bicarbonate of soda, *1 teaspoon*

Fresh buttermilk or milk, *300ml (½ pint)*

1 Preheat the oven to 230°C/450°F/Gas 8. Dust a baking sheet with a little flour.

2 Mix together the wholemeal and white flours, salt and bicarbonate of soda in a large mixing bowl. Stir in the buttermilk or milk and mix together to make a soft dough.

3 Turn the dough out on to a floured surface and knead lightly for a few moments. Soda bread doesn't require the same amount of kneading that ordinary bread does – just a minute or two is all that's necessary.

4 Shape the dough into a round and dust with flour. Lift on to the prepared baking sheet and cut a deep cross in the top of the loaf.

5 Bake in the oven for about 35–40 minutes. Remove from the oven and allow the loaf to cool for a couple of minutes, then take it off the baking sheet and wrap it loosely in a clean tea towel so that the crust stays softer.

COOK'S TIP:

▨ You can often find buttermilk in the chill cabinet at health food shops and supermarkets – though if you have trouble finding it, just use milk instead.

PINEAPPLE AND CHERRY TEA BREAD

You'll love this wonderful tea bread. It's moist and fruity, and tastes delicious plain or spread with butter.

SERVES 8–12

Suitable for vegetarians • Suitable for freezing

Ready-to-eat dried exotic fruit, *225g (8oz), roughly chopped*

Fruit tea bags, *2*

Butter, *75g (3oz)*

Golden caster sugar, *110g (4oz)*

Self-raising flour, *175g (6oz)*

Salt, *pinch*

Eggs, *2, beaten*

Pineapple pieces in natural juice, *1 x 227g can, drained*

Glacé cherries, *50g (2oz), halved*

1 Put the ready-to-eat dried fruit into a large heatproof bowl and pour in just enough boiling water to cover it. Add the fruit tea bags, stir, then cover and leave to soak for at least 1 hour. Drain well.

2 Put the butter and sugar into a large saucepan and heat gently until melted. Add the drained fruit and cook over a low heat, stirring often,

for 3–4 minutes. Transfer to a mixing bowl and allow to cool completely.

3 Preheat the oven to 180°C/350°F/Gas 4. Grease and line a 900g (2lb) loaf tin.

4 Sift the flour and salt into the cooled fruit mixture and stir well. Add the eggs, pineapple pieces and cherries. Stir well. Transfer to the prepared tin.

5 Bake for 50 minutes–1 hour. Test the cake with a fine skewer: if it comes out clean, the cake is cooked. If not, return to the oven for a few more minutes.

COOK'S TIP:

▓ Use ready-to-eat dried orchard fruits instead of the exotic variety, or simply use a combination of sultanas and raisins.

ROSEMARY, ONION AND CHEDDAR FOCACCIA

Baking with yeast is very therapeutic and the results are delicious, so try this wonderful savoury focaccia – it's a very tasty Italian-style bread, perfect served with cheese and pickles for a snack or light lunch.

MAKES 2

Suitable for vegetarians • Suitable for freezing

Strong plain white flour, *750g (1lb 11oz)*

Salt, *1 teaspoon*

Easy-blend yeast, *1 sachet (11g)*

Mature Cheddar cheese, *110g (4oz), grated*

Freshly ground black pepper

Milk, *150ml (¼ pint)*

Boiling water, *300ml (½ pint)*

Butter, *25g (1oz), cut into pieces*

Red onion, *1 large, thinly sliced*

Sun-dried tomatoes, *50g (2oz), torn into thin strips*

Rosemary sprigs, *a few*

Black and green olives, *about 20*

Olive oil, *2 tablespoons*

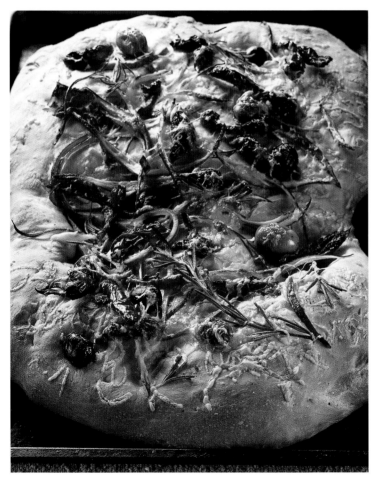

1 Sift the flour and salt into a very large mixing bowl. Add the yeast and half the Cheddar cheese. Season with black pepper and stir well to combine. Mix the milk and boiling water together to give a hand-hot temperature, then add the butter and allow it to melt. Stir into the flour and mix with your hands to make a soft dough.

2 Turn the dough on to a floured surface and knead for about 5 minutes until smooth. Place in a lightly oiled bowl and cover with a damp cloth or cling film. Leave to rise in a warm, draught-free place until doubled in size. This should take about 1 hour.

3 Lightly oil two baking sheets. Knock back the dough and knead it lightly for a few seconds. Cut into two equal pieces, then roll out each piece on a floured surface to fit the baking sheets. Cover loosely with a damp cloth or cling film and leave to rise for about 20 minutes.

4 Meanwhile, preheat the oven to 200°C/400°F/Gas 6.

5 Scatter the red onion, sun-dried tomatoes, rosemary, olives and remaining cheese over the top of the two focaccia. Drizzle with the olive oil, then bake for 15–20 minutes until risen and golden.

COOK'S TIPS:

▓ The time that the dough takes to rise will depend upon the conditions. If your kitchen is very warm, it will rise quite quickly, though it will take longer if the surroundings are cooler.

▓ If using sun-dried tomatoes in olive oil, use 2 tablespoons of the oil from the jar for drizzling over the focaccia before baking, to add more flavour.

▓ Wrap and freeze one of the focaccia to use another time.

children's favourites

Mini Pancakes oozing with golden syrup, Crunchie Banana Splits and Strawberry Yogurt Shakes, – these are children's favourites that we never grow out of. Whether you're cooking for youngsters or looking for recipes that children can give you a hand with, this is the chapter for you.

It's a great idea to get children involved with cooking, for the chances are they'll get involved with the eating too. That way they just might grow up with an avid interest in the things they eat, and a healthy enthusiasm for preparing something that's good for them. It's worth remembering that children really benefit from including milk and dairy products in their diet – and the same goes for adults too – so enjoy your daily quota.

Getting the hang of...

MINI PANCAKES WITH GOLDEN SYRUP

This is one of those brilliant recipes to make when the children are hungry and they want something filling and fun to eat. With a few store-cupboard ingredients, you can knock up a thick batter for making these mini pancakes, which are also known as drop scones or Scotch pancakes. Traditionally, they were made by dropping spoonfuls of batter onto a hot griddle – hence the name – though you can make them in a frying pan with a heavy base.

Here a combination of natural yogurt and milk is used to make the batter, but you could use just milk or cultured buttermilk instead. The consistency you are aiming for is quite thick, similar to that of double cream. Serve the pancakes with golden syrup, or simply spread them with butter and strawberry jam. You could even add a handful of sultanas or raisins to the batter mixture, if you like. Whichever way you make them, this is a recipe well worth getting the hang of.

All children love pancakes, especially when they're drizzled with oodles of golden syrup. Besides, they're so easy to make, the kids can give you a hand. So why not make a stack of them today?

SERVES 4

Suitable for vegetarians

Self-raising flour, *110g (4oz)*	
Salt, *pinch*	
Golden caster sugar, *15g (½oz)*	
Egg, *1 large*	
Vanilla extract, *1 teaspoon*	
Natural yogurt, *150g (5oz)*	
Milk, *2 tablespoons*	
Vegetable oil, *2–3 teaspoons*	
Golden syrup, *to serve*	

1   Sift the flour and salt into a large bowl and stir in the sugar. Crack the egg into the middle, then add the vanilla extract, yogurt and milk. Beat together with a wire whisk to make a smooth, thick batter.

2   Next, heat a pancake pan – ideally, it should be very heavy with shallow sides. Add a few drops of vegetable oil. Turn the heat to low, then drop tablespoonfuls of the batter into the hot pan, allowing room for them to spread.

3   Cook over a medium heat until bubbles appear and the surface of the batter just begins to set – this will take about 2 minutes. Flip the pancakes over with a palette knife to cook the other sides.

4   Cook the pancakes until golden brown, then lift out onto sheets of kitchen paper. Keep them in a warm place whilst you cook the remaining batter, adding a few more drops of oil to the pan when needed.

5   Serve the pancakes when they are warm, drizzled with lots of golden syrup, or spread with butter and jam.

COOK'S TIP:

▪ If you like sultanas or raisins, add about 25g (1oz) to the batter before you cook the pancakes.

FRUIT CHUNKS DUNKED IN HOT CHOC DIP

Some of the easiest things to make are absolutely wonderful to eat. You'll just love this recipe!

SERVES 4

Suitable for vegetarians

Fresh fruit, *to serve (e.g. bananas, strawberries, kiwi fruit, apples)*	
Plain chocolate, *110g (4oz), broken into pieces*	
Golden syrup, *3 tablespoons*	
Cocoa powder, *3 tablespoons*	
Cornflour, *1 tablespoon*	
Milk, *250ml (8fl oz)*	

1 First of all, prepare your chosen fruit by cutting it carefully into bite-sized pieces. Share it out between four serving plates or bowls.
2 Next, make the hot chocolate dip. Put the chocolate, golden syrup, cocoa powder, cornflour and milk into a heavy-based saucepan. Heat gently over a low heat, stirring constantly with a wooden spoon, until thickened, smooth and glossy.
3 Pour the dip into one large bowl, for sharing, or 4 small bowls to serve with each portion of the fruit.

COOK'S TIP:

▨ Try not to let the chocolate sauce boil too much. Once it has thickened, turn off the heat.

VANILLA FRAPPACCINO

A cross between an iced coffee and a cappuccino, this chilled drink tastes absolutely divine.

SERVES 2

Suitable for vegetarians

Instant coffee powder or granules, *2 rounded teaspoons*	
Dark or light muscovado sugar, *2 rounded teaspoons*	
Double or whipping cream, *5 tablespoons*	
Milk, *600ml (1 pint)*	
Vanilla extract, *1 teaspoon*	
Vanilla dairy ice cream, *4 scoops*	
Cocoa powder, *for sprinkling*	

1 Dissolve the instant coffee and sugar in a very small amount of boiling water. Leave to cool whilst you whip the cream until it holds its shape.
2 Put the coffee mixture into a blender or food processor with half the whipped cream and the milk, vanilla extract and 2 scoops of ice cream. Whizz together for 15–20 seconds until blended and frothy.
3 Pour the mixture into 2 large mugs, top each one with a dollop of whipped cream and a scoop of ice cream, then serve, sprinkled with a little cocoa powder.

COOK'S TIP:

▨ You don't have to make the drinks in a blender or food processor – you could simply whisk the ingredients together with a wire whisk.

BANANA AND RASPBERRY MILK FLOAT

Bananas make fabulous milk shakes, especially when topped with a scoop of vanilla dairy ice cream!

SERVES 4

Suitable for vegetarians

Milk, *900ml (1½ pints)*

Bananas, *2 large or 3 small*

Natural yogurt, *150g (5oz)*

Vanilla extract, *2 teaspoons*

Vanilla dairy ice cream, *8 scoops*

Raspberry or strawberry syrup topping

Raspberries, *110g (4oz), defrosted if frozen*

1 Put the milk, bananas, yogurt, vanilla and 4 scoops of ice cream into a blender or food processor, then whizz together for 15–20 seconds until smooth.
2 Squeeze or spoon a little raspberry or strawberry syrup into the base of four glasses. Add a few raspberries, reserving some for decoration, then top up with the banana milk shake mixture – allowing some room for the last scoops of ice cream.
3 Top each drink with the remaining ice cream and decorate with the reserved raspberries and a drizzle of the raspberry or strawberry syrup. Serve at once, with a spoon!

COOK'S TIP:

Cold milk for drinking should always be served well-chilled, so bear that in mind when making milk shakes.

HOT CHOCOLATE WITH MELTING MARSHMALLOWS

Curl up on the sofa with one of these delicious hot chocolate drinks – they're a real treat for kids of all ages!

SERVES 4

Suitable for vegetarians

Milk, *1.2 litres (2 pints)*

Drinking chocolate, *4 rounded tablespoons*

Ground cinnamon, *pinch (optional)*

Mini marshmallows, *to decorate*

Chocolate flake, *1, to decorate*

1 Put the milk in a saucepan with the drinking chocolate and cinnamon, if using. Heat, whisking with a small wire whisk, until almost boiling. This gives the hot chocolate a deliciously frothy finish.
2 Pour the mixture into mugs or heatproof glasses and pile the mini marshmallows on top. Crumble the chocolate flake and sprinkle it over the drinks. Serve immediately.

COOK'S TIPS:

For extra creaminess, add a couple of tablespoons of single, whipping or double cream to the milk before heating.

Make the drink for one with 300ml (½ pint) of milk and one tablespoon of drinking chocolate. You'll just have to eat the rest of the chocolate flake yourself.

STRAWBERRY YOGURT SHAKES

Whizz together some fresh strawberries, fresh cream, milk and strawberry yogurt to make some fantastic milk shakes.

SERVES 4

Suitable for vegetarians

Double or whipping cream, *4 tablespoons*

Strawberries, *350g (12oz), stalks removed*

Thick and creamy strawberry yogurt, *2 x 150g (5oz) pots*

Strawberry jam, *3 tablespoons*

Milk, *900ml (1½ pints)*

1 Whip the cream in a chilled bowl until it holds its shape. Set aside whilst you make the drinks.

2 Reserve a few slices of strawberry for decoration, then put the rest into a blender or food processor. Add the yogurt, strawberry jam and milk, then blend for about 15–20 seconds until smooth.

3 Pour into 4 glasses and decorate with the whipped cream and strawberries. Serve at once or cover and chill in the refrigerator for 20–30 minutes, where the milk shakes will thicken slightly.

COOK'S TIP:

▓ Add a banana to the blender for more thickness and flavour.

CHERRY JELLIES

Simple to make and tasty to eat – children will love these jellies. Why not make lots next time you throw a party for them?

SERVES 4

Boiling water, *300ml (½ pint)*

Raspberry or strawberry jelly crystals, *1 sachet*

Cherries, *110g (4oz)*

Double or whipping cream, *150 ml (¼ pint)*

1 Pour the boiling water into a measuring jug and sprinkle in the jelly crystals, stirring them until they dissolve. Add 250ml (8fl oz) of cold water to the mixture to make it up to 550ml (18fl oz) in total.

2 Pour the jelly mixture into four glasses. Reserve a few cherries for decoration, then cut the rest in half and remove their stones. Divide them between the jellies, then transfer them to the refrigerator to set. This will take between 1–2 hours.

3 When ready to serve, whip the cream in a chilled bowl until it holds its shape. Spoon onto the jellies and decorate with the reserved cherries.

COOK'S TIPS:

▓ Use strawberries or raspberries instead of cherries, or use orange flavour jelly crystals and drained canned mandarins for a change.

▓ When the jellies have set, try topping them with a layer of thick and creamy cherry yogurt before you spoon the cream on top.

CHOCOLATE CRISPY CAKES

These yummy chocolate crispy cakes are fun to make, and they're such a treat to eat!

MAKES ABOUT 12

Plain or milk chocolate, *200g (7oz)*

Butter, *25g (1oz)*

Cornflakes or rice crispies, *75g (3oz)*

Smarties or mini marshmallows, *25g (1oz)*

1   Break up the chocolate into squares and cut the butter into pieces, then put them into a large heatproof bowl.
2   Carefully position the bowl over a large saucepan that has about 10cm (4 inches) of gently simmering water in it. Allow the chocolate and butter to melt, stirring it every so often with a wooden spoon until the mixture is smooth. Turn off the heat and put the bowl on to a work surface, taking care, as the bowl will be hot.
3   Add the cornflakes or rice crispies to the chocolate mixture, stirring gently so that they are coated with it.
4   Spoon the mixture into paper bun cases, then decorate them with some Smarties or mini marshmallows. Put the cakes on to a plate and chill them in the refrigerator until they have set. This will take about 20 minutes.

FRENCH TOAST WITH BANANAS AND MAPLE SYRUP

The perfect snack for hungry children when they arrive home from school – or serve it for breakfast for a filling, nutritious start to the day.

SERVES 2

Suitable for vegetarians

White bread, *2 thick slices*	
Egg, *1*	
Milk, *150ml (¼ pint)*	
Vanilla extract, *1 teaspoon*	
Butter, *25g (1oz)*	
Maple or golden syrup, *5 tablespoons*	
Bananas, *2 small, sliced*	

1   Cut the crusts off the bread, then cut each slice in half diagonally to make two triangles.
2   In a large shallow bowl, beat together the egg, milk and vanilla extract. Add the pieces of bread to the mixture and leave them to soak for about 5 minutes. Turn them over once so that both sides get a good soaking.
3   Heat the butter in a large frying pan until it has melted, but be careful not to let it burn. Add the soaked bread and fry gently for about 1 or 2 minutes until it has set and turned golden brown. Turn over the pieces and cook them on the other side for another minute or two.
4   Push the bread to one side of the frying pan. Spoon in the syrup and add the sliced bananas. Heat and bubble up the mixture for about 30 seconds, then remove from the heat.
5   Divide the French toast, bananas and syrup between 2 warm plates and tuck in at once.

COOK'S TIP:

■ For a special treat, serve with a scoop of dairy ice cream or a dollop of fresh cream.

CRUNCHIE BANANA SPLIT

Banana split is one of the quickest and easiest desserts to put together. It's fun to make, and fantastic to eat!

SERVES 4

Suitable for vegetarians

Double cream, *150ml (¼ pint)*

Bananas, *4*

Dairy vanilla ice cream, *12 small scoops*

Strawberries or raspberries, *350g (12oz), sliced if large*

Crunchie chocolate bar, *1 standard size, roughly crushed*

Strawberry syrup topping, *to decorate*

1   Chill a large mixing bowl in the refrigerator or freezer for about 5 minutes. Add the cream and whip it with a hand-held whisk until it holds its shape. Put it into a piping bag fitted with a star nozzle, if you like, or just set it to one side for a few minutes whilst you assemble the bananas.

2   Peel and slice the bananas lengthways, then sandwich each one of them together on separate serving dishes with three scoops of vanilla ice cream.

3   Scatter the strawberries or raspberries over the split bananas and top with piped rosettes or spoonfuls of the whipped cream.

4   Sprinkle with crushed Crunchie and drizzle with strawberry syrup. Serve at once. Yum!

COOK'S TIP:

▓   Allow the ice cream to soften in the refrigerator for about 10–15 minutes before you scoop it out, otherwise it will be very difficult to serve.

EASY CHEESY PUDDINGS

These little savoury puddings come out of the oven all puffed up and golden brown, and they taste superb.

SERVES 4

Suitable for vegetarians

Butter, *50g (2oz)*

Bread, *8 slices from a medium or thin-sliced loaf*

Onion, *1 small, finely chopped*

Cheddar cheese, *150g (5oz), finely grated*

Eggs, *2*

Milk, *450ml (¾ pint)*

Salt and freshly ground black pepper

1 Preheat the oven to 180°C/350°F/Gas 4. Find an ovenproof baking dish that has a capacity of about 1.5 litre (2½ pints), or use 4 individual baking dishes. Use a little bit of the butter to grease them.

2 Using a small round biscuit cutter, stamp out as many circles as possible from the slices of bread. Layer half of these circles in the baking dish or dishes.

3 Melt the rest of the butter in a small saucepan and add the onion. Fry it gently, stirring it with a wooden spoon, until it has softened. This will take about 3 minutes. When it is golden, tip it over the bread in the baking dish or individual dishes.

4 Sprinkle half the grated cheese over the onion. Neatly layer the rest of the bread circles over the cheese.

5 Beat the eggs in a large jug, then add the milk and beat again. Season with some salt and pepper. Pour this mixture carefully over the bread in the baking dishes. Leave it to soak in for about 10 minutes.

6 Sprinkle the rest of the cheese evenly over the top of the bread, then carefully transfer the dishes to the oven. Bake for 30–40 minutes, until the puddings have risen up and turned golden brown.

COOK'S TIP:

▦ Don't worry when the puddings deflate after you take them out of the oven – they will still taste fantastic.

CHEESE AND TOMATO TARTS

So easy to make as they use ready-rolled puff pastry, these tarts are best eaten whilst warm – a few minutes after they come out of the oven.

SERVES 6

Suitable for vegetarians • Suitable for freezing

Ready-rolled puff pastry sheet, *1 x 375g (13oz), defrosted if frozen*

Mature Cheddar cheese, *110g (4oz), grated*

Tomatoes, *6 small, halved*

Mixed dried herbs, *2 teaspoons*

Salt and freshly ground black pepper

Beaten egg or milk, *to glaze*

1 Preheat the oven to 200°C/400°F/Gas 6. Lightly grease a large baking sheet.

2 Unroll the puff pastry sheet and cut into six equal rectangles. Using a sharp knife, score a border within each pastry rectangle about 2cm (¾ inch) from the edge, being careful to avoid cutting right through the pastry. Place on the baking sheet.

3 Sprinkle the cheese into the middle of each rectangle. Arrange the tomato halves on top, then sprinkle with the dried herbs and season with salt and pepper.

4 Brush the pastry edges with beaten egg or milk, then bake for about 20 minutes, until the cheese is bubbling and golden and the pastry is risen and crisp. Cool for a few minutes, then serve.

COOK'S TIP:

▦ Add chopped cooked ham or pepperoni and finely sliced spring onions to the filling for a tasty variation.

TOADS-IN-THE-HOLES

Make these mini versions of toad-in-the-hole for a meal or snack that children and adults will enjoy.

SERVES 4

Plain flour, *110g (4oz)*	
Salt, *¼ teaspoon*	
Egg, *1*	
Milk, *300ml (½ pint)*	
Cocktail sausages, *12*	
Vegetable oil, *6 teaspoons*	

1   Sift the flour and salt into a large bowl and crack the egg into the middle. Add the milk, all at once, and beat well with a hand whisk to make a smooth batter. Pour the batter into a jug and let it stand whilst the oven heats up.

2   Preheat the oven to 220°C/425°F/Gas 7.

3   Pop the sausages into a deep 12-hole bun tin and add ½ teaspoon of oil to each one. Put into the oven for 5 minutes, so that the oil is very hot.

4   Do this next bit as quickly as possible. Remove the bun tin from the oven, pour a little batter around each sausage and return to the oven as quickly as possible. Shut the oven door swiftly, and keep it shut for the next 25 minutes. Take a quick peek after 25 minutes, and if necessary cook for an extra 5 minutes or so until the toads are well-risen and golden brown.

COOK'S TIP:

▓ Avoid opening the oven door too soon, or else the toads might not rise.

TASTY TOASTIES

It's easy to forget how delicious toasted sandwiches can be – but just wait until you catch the wonderful smells as they cook – then you'll remember!

SERVES 2

Suitable for vegetarians

Medium sliced white bread, *4 slices from a large loaf*	
Butter, *for spreading*	
Mature Cheddar cheese, *50g (2oz), grated*	
Spring onions, *2, finely chopped*	
Chutney and cucumber or tomatoes, *to serve*	

1   Preheat a toasted sandwich maker whilst you prepare the sandwiches.

2   Cut the crusts from the bread and spread the slices thinly with butter. Flip the slices over – the filling goes on the unbuttered side – and divide the cheese and spring onions between two slices. Top with the remaining bread – buttered side outside.

3   Cook the sandwiches in the sandwich toaster – they will take about 5 minutes, though check after about 3 minutes to see how they are getting on. Cook until golden brown.

4   Cool the sandwiches for a minute or two as the filling can be very hot, then serve them with chutney and cucumber or tomatoes.

COOK'S TIPS:

▓ If you don't have a toasted sandwich maker, just grill the sandwiches on each side until golden brown.

▓ Choose your favourite filling for these tasty toasted sandwiches – ham and tomato, corned beef and pickled onion, cheese and chutney – whatever you like.

LITTLE PIZZAS

Pizzas always go down well, whether it's for snacks, picnics or parties. These mini versions are perfect for smaller appetites.

SERVES 6

Suitable for freezing

Self-raising flour, *300g (11oz)*

Salt, *½ level teaspoon*

Butter, *75g (3oz), cut into pieces*

Milk, *150ml (¼ pint)*

Tomato pizza topping, *1 small jar*

Italian mixed dried herbs, *1 tablespoon*

Tomatoes, *3, sliced*

Cheddar cheese, *75g (3oz), grated*

Cooked ham, *50g (2oz), chopped*

Pineapple chunks in natural juice, *1 x 200g can, drained*

Salt and freshly ground black pepper

1   Check that the shelves in the oven are positioned towards the top, then set the oven temperature to 200°C/400°F/Gas 6.

2   Sift the flour and salt into a large mixing bowl. Add the butter and rub it in to the flour using the tips of your fingers. Stop when there are no lumps of butter left.

3   Mix the milk into the flour mixture with a fork, then use your hands to bring the mixture together into a ball. Be careful not to add too much milk – the dough should be soft, but not sticky. Knead it for a few seconds so that it is smooth.

4   Divide the dough into six equal pieces and roll into balls. Sprinkle a work surface and a rolling pin with a little flour, then roll out each piece of dough into a circle about 10cm (4 inches) in diameter. Place them onto lightly greased baking sheets.

5   Spread the pizza topping thinly over the surface of the dough circles. Sprinkle with a few dried herbs, then top with tomato slices, grated cheese, ham and pineapple. Season with a little salt and pepper.

6   Bake the pizzas in the oven for 15–20 minutes. Allow them to cool for a few minutes, then tuck in!

COOK'S TIPS:

▩ Try your own favourite toppings – pepperoni sausage, mushroom, crispy bacon or extra cheese – the choice is yours.

▩ If you have any pineapple left over, serve on cocktail sticks with chunks of cheese.

INDEX